Writing Baseball

THE SOUTHERN ILLINOIS UNIVERSITY PRESS SERIES

Other Books in the Writing Baseball Series

LINE DRIVES

100 Contemporary Baseball Poems

EDITED BY

Brooke Horvath

AND

Tim Wiles

WITH A FOREWORD BY
ELINOR NAUEN

**SOUTHERN ILLINOIS
UNIVERSITY PRESS**

Carbondale and Edwardsville

Library of Congress Cataloging-in-Publication Data

Line drives : 100 contemporary baseball poems / edited by Brooke Horvath and
Tim Wiles ; with a foreword by Elinor Nauen.
    p. cm. — (Writing baseball)
    Includes bibliographical references.
    1. Baseball—Poetry. 2. Baseball players—Poetry. 3. American
poetry—20th century. I. Horvath, Brooke. II. Wiles, Tim, 1964– III. Series.
ISBN 0-8093-2439-3 (alk. paper)
ISBN 0-8093-2440-7 (pbk. : alk. paper)
PS595.B33 L55 2002
811'.6080355—dc21   2001042909

Writing Baseball Series Editor: RICHARD PETERSON

For my mother, Nancy Horvath,
who taught me poetry,
and my father, Eugene Horvath,
who taught me baseball—
with thanks
for never criticizing my skill
at either.
—B. H.

For Susan Becker
—T. W.

Contents

Contents

Two

Three

Contents

Five

Contents

Foreword

Elinor Nauen

The other afternoon, I took the manuscript for *Line Drives* to a park near my house, where I watched some five-year-olds play T-ball. Although unskilled, the kids already had an idea of the moves and stances that would become baseball. *It was* baseball, in fact. Here and from nearby diamonds were familiar noises — encouragement and groans, along with a few more chuckles than you generally hear at major-league ball parks. I sat and watched and thought about how language becomes poetry. From hesitant beginnings, with the moves and stances inchoate but apparent, comes the grace of the game, the beauty of the poem.

What is it about baseball and poetry? Why do they go together like 60 feet and 6 inches? In "The Retarded Children Play Baseball," Wesley McNair writes:

> Forget the coaches shouting back
> about the way the game is played
>
> and consider the game
> they're already playing, or playing
> perhaps elsewhere on some other field,
>
> like the shortstop, who stands transfixed
> all through the action, staring
> at what appears to be nothing.

In a way, poets are the slow children, seeing what others don't but with the ability to say what these children can't—to talk of the layers of meaning wrapped inside their heads and around the outside of the field, where "the horsehide . . . skips off the nap of the close-clipped turf / as if it were still on the horse" (Caron Andregg, "Solid Single").

Maybe the question is: Why do poets so famously like baseball? So much baseball literature, so little from any other sport. For one thing, baseball is leisurely enough that even the most attentive watcher of the game still has time for thought. It also has the physical beauty (a clean line drive single, young men's muscles) that all poets are obsessed with. It's intricate and shapely, like a good poem.

There's nothing more American than baseball—we all know that—the fiercely independent, light-filled America that's both real and imagined: it's the best that can be imagined and the reality that can be created with a few words: "With an old glove like this and a new baseball, / you could start the whole world over" writes Ron McFarland in "Why I Love Baseball." And Karen Zaborowski and her daughter find themselves, in "World Series, Game 5," in "probably the two worst seats at the Vet / but right where the whole world / wants to be." What else do you need to know?

Now, I love baseball and I love poetry, but I often don't love baseball poems. Too many are too full of too much cheap nostalgia, where the poet thinks that by mentioning some old-time player or famous homer, he's done the work of creating an emotion or connection. Baseball somehow makes poets unafraid to speak of love, but too often it blossoms as sentimentality.

The poems of *Line Drives* avoid these common traps. They can and do hit the curve. While plenty poignant, full of distant fathers and lost childhoods, these poems are clear-eyed. Sentiment is earned; there's tenderness without gush. The poems in this collection bring us back to many forgotten rituals, ghost runners and "A handful of us kicking through the weeds / beyond the edge of the field, looking for / the lost baseball" (Richard Behm, "Looking for the Baseball"). They bring in other worlds without disrupting the world of the game. They take us to the Mediterranean and Detroit on Polish-American night, to St. Louis and Southeast Asia, to the World Series and spring training, to a Bud-

dhist college, Lake Superior and Joseph A. Soldati's "hot hushed eve-
nings of July" by way of food, jokes, jazz, Dante (twice), Dizzy Dean,
Baudelaire, Geronimo, Bud Powell, Satchel Paige, Proust, Jane Austen,
a lunar eclipse, and a big handful of ball parks — major-league, minor-
league, not-really, and no-longer.

Fans like nothing better than talking about baseball, and in this
book is talk of the highest order. "He sees it happen and imagines it— /
The same thing really," writes Baron Wormser. A good baseball poem
(like a good poem on any topic) serves up easy moments as well as a
knee-buckling curve once in a while. When you're too nervous to watch
(two on, two behind, two out, two strikes), dip into these poems and
you'll be able to stand it. When your spouse says accusingly, "All you
care about is the Yankees"— and you know that if you, as in Kathryn
Dunn's poem, had just twenty-four hours to live, you'd want to spend at
least part of it driving down the FDR with the windows down, listening
to the game on the radio — these poems will justify and dignify your de-
sire (and the probable dissolution of your marriage).

I checked off so many of these poems to mention as favorites that it
got ridiculous. Added one name after another to my list of "poets to read
more of." I kept finding lines that seemed the perfect emblem for all of
them, which is as silly as announcing that today's game stands for all of
baseball. Each is itself, each has its own exact moment of beauty — the
shortstop leaping over a sliding runner to turn the double play, "they'll
believe their love / was the difference, not the simple grace of / the cen-
ter fielder's glove" (George Looney, "Tired of Loss and Sin"). The satis-
fied swing and satisfying thwonk, an archetypal moment of thought. In
the end, I refrained from picking a highlights tape, knowing that a barn-
burner line doesn't make the poem, any more than one swing makes the
game, knowing that readers want to find their own. I'm amazed that
there's always more to say, metaphors that haven't been used before.

However, I do have to say I'm particularly glad the editors appreci-
ate the short poem — for example, Larry Zirlin's funny, sad, and exact
"Last Baseball Dream of the Season," which ends the book. Even in his
dreams, the poet says, he's batting only .241— and that is "everything"
you need to know about him. In Jeff Worley's somewhat longer "Bio-
graphical Note," memoir meets Napoleonic necessity, recapitulating

history without grandiosity. These two poems accomplish what the *Baseball Encyclopedia* does so magically in laying out "everything" with a line of numbers.

We know, of course, that the time of a game persists for as long as there's an out left. We sometimes forget that all baseball, like all poetry, takes place at the same time, an eternal now. We can watch Clemente again, or Walter Johnson for the first time, or really fix Killebrew's swing in memory. Robert Gibb, in "Williams in Autumn" (and that's William Carlos, not Ted) mentions "figures / Who are about to step out of Eden / Into the world of time." You are luckier — you are about to step out of the world of time into the Eden of these hundred terrific poems.

Editors' Acknowledgments

We would like to thank Richard Peterson, Writing Baseball series editor, and Karl Kageff of Southern Illinois University Press for their expert guidance as this project made its way over the course of several years from idea to book. Thanks, too, to Don Johnson for his helpful comments along the way (and for providing a model of excellence in his *Hummers, Knucklers, and Slow Curves*) and to Kathy Brand of the Kent State University's Stark Campus library for her help with our computer searches.

Thanks as well to everyone who took the time to recommend and, upon occasion, to track down and send to us copies of favorite baseball poems; special thanks here to Paul Bauer of Archer's Books in Kent, Ohio, for locating obscure materials for us.

Thanks to all the poets who didn't know us or send us a thing but who have kindly allowed their work to be included here and to their publishers for granting permission to reprint. We are especially indebted to those poets and presses who generously waived or reduced their normal reprint fees.

Particular thanks to everyone who submitted work. We were gratified by the copious response to our call for poems, are pleased to have been able to include everyone whose poetry is collected here, and wish there had been room for more of you.

Brooke Horvath wishes to thank Tim Wiles for never resorting to what any sane man would have done — getting in his car, driving from Cooperstown to Ohio, and shooting his coeditor for being such a difficult-to-please nuisance.

Editors' Acknowledgments

Tim Wiles wishes to thank Brooke Horvath (he was vague as to why) as well as to pass along his personal thanks to Richard Peterson, Karl Kageff, and the whole gang at SIU Press. Finally, Tim sends thanks to Lori Kammerdiner, Mike and Linda Schacht, Mikhail Horowitz, Mike Shannon, Tom Goldstein, Ben Caffyn, Dan Stein, Tom Heitz, Jim Gates, Joe Wallace, Christine Buslon, Eliot Asinof, and the mailroom crew at the Baseball Hall of Fame for putting up with thousands of submissions: John Horne, Jen Taylor, and Jon "Beamish" Blomquist.

Finally, both editors wish to thank the University Research Council of Kent State University for kindly providing the funds necessary to buy the rights to reprint several of the poems included herein.

Editors' Introduction

Here is a story we believe we remember. It must have been 1979 because Pete Rose was making one of his rare appearances at third for Philadelphia. We don't recall who the opposing team was, but their third-base coach was wired for sound so everyone watching at home could hear the wisdom routinely dispensed at the hot corner.

"Hey, Pete!" the coach called out late in the game, "we took a vote last night on who was the best-looking Phillie."

Rose tossed a look his way but otherwise remained preoccupied with the business perhaps soon to be in hand.

"You came in second!"

Now the master of distraction had Rose's attention. "Really?" Rose asked incredulously.

"Yeah . . . the rest of your team tied for first!"

We tell this story because it sometimes seems that no matter how good a baseball poem is, some will always feel that baseball as subject matter relegates a poem to also-ran status. Perhaps this is the unfortunate legacy of "Casey at the Bat," that poem forever on the barroom floor somewhere in the foothills of Parnassus.[1] Yet as the poet William Matthews has observed, to speak in terms of subject matter is somehow never to speak adequately of poetry, which chooses its provisional subject "in order that it be transformed" (143), that it provide the occasion for passionate attention and articulate reflection.

If poetry is an occasion for well-put passion and expressive pondering, so also is baseball, as every fan knows. Just such attention as transmutes the prose of everyday life into poetry transforms as well this game we read or write about, play or watch. Or does if we let it: as the essayist

John Hildebidle has reflected, baseball's principal allure for the mature fan "lies not in what occurs on the field . . . but in the forces of memory and imagination" (180), which infuse the game with whatever significance and pleasure we are able to make it yield. If Hildebidle is correct, then baseball is like much else here at the start of a new millennium when so much of what we thought we knew seems suddenly riddled with doubt, when too much seems to mean only and whatever we can make it mean, and when sense making too often seems a dicey undertaking. But perhaps this is why baseball offers us welcome relief: neither because it is meaningless or unserious nor because it lends itself to easy reading, but because it offers an inviting, threat-free subject upon which to exercise the mind's analytic, interpretive, and evaluative proclivities. Or say that we welcome the game because, in the words of Jacques Barzun, it is our "true realm of clear ideas" (160).

Moreover, although the game may (and frequently does) lead us into profoundly consequential topics, as the poems gathered here testify, to think about the game is always somehow to be thinking about play and remains at its best a playful activity — much like poetry making itself. It is indeed the case that the seriously intellectual sportiveness inspired by baseball can produce such creativity and insight that for the thinking fan the game routinely becomes about as profound as things get. At the same time, the need to transform these materials into poetry gives recollection shape and enfranchises imagination. Indeed, what we hope you will find in the pages of this anthology are poems that supply baseball both with heretofore unexpected depths and with surprising but apt connections to what lies beyond the ball park, even as your reasons for having loved the game are given voice and confirmed.

Well-made poems, at any rate, that take us deeply into baseball while allowing it to take us deeply into much else; poems that assiduously avoid the dull and the already-said; poems that line after line, like baseball itself game after game and season after season, manage to make the old and the familiar insightfully new and surprising: such are the poems we have sought to include in *Line Drives*.

The one hundred selections comprising this collection were chosen from over four thousand poems either submitted by their authors in response to a call that ran in sundry magazines or gathered through computer searches, from our files, at the suggestion of friends and other poets, and by combing back issues of several sport and baseball magazines.[2] Our goal was to offer a collection that was different from the several that have preceded ours, and indeed one of our principal selection guidelines was to include no poem already available in previous baseball or sport-literature anthologies.[3] We wished as well to assemble as various a collection as possible, one that presented the work of as many poets as could be accommodated; for this reason we limited the number of poems by any one poet to two, and the number of poets represented by two poems to a handful. In the process, we have made room for established authors and for poets whose names will be new to most readers of this collection; for poems in any style and on any subject; for poems both serious and humorous; for poems keen on taking us deeply into baseball as sport and poems intent on using the game as a metaphor for exploring history, religion, love, family, self-identity, and much more.

Beyond the desire to collect previously unanthologized work, we decided against the inclusion of poetry for children and young adults; parodies, reworkings, and other poems whose success depended heavily upon acquaintance with other work;[4] poems in which the baseball content was inaccurate;[5] and excerpts from poems too long to include in their entirety. This last decision accounts for the absence of several otherwise admirable poems from poetic sequences when we felt these poems required the context of their companions for full effect.[6] It is also the case that we had finally to omit more than a few poems either because we could not locate their authors to ask for permission to include their work or because we could not afford the permission fees involved.

If the editors of an anthology are analogous to the manager of a team, it was our difficult task to select from many talented players those who would take the field. Although we have included some poetry in prose, we considered no prose that was not meant to be read as poetry. Following tradition, we considered and have included poems about softball. Finally, although it was tempting to select poems with an eye toward developing themes throughout the course of the book, of telling cumulatively a larger, unified story or forwarding some hundred-poem argument about the game, we have elected rather to include here whatever struck us as provocative, fresh, funny, well done; poems that were fun to read aloud or that made us want to share them with others; poems that repaid rereading and that we enjoyed revisiting.

"We wait for baseball all winter long," Bill Littlefield wrote in *Boston Magazine* a decade ago, "or rather, we remember it and anticipate it at the same time. We re-create what we have known and we imagine what we are going to see next. Maybe that's what poets do, too" (71). It is certainly what we did as editors of this book—waited and remembered, anticipated and imagined—and, like fans and poets, we did some cheering and a fair amount of agonizing, arguing, and second-guessing. But we did all this, finally, for the same reason Littlefield suspects poets write of baseball: "because it feels good" (71). That being the case, there is no use trying to disguise the fact that, finally and most honestly, we picked poems we liked.

Line Drives speaks of many things: of murder and ghost runners and old ball gloves; baseball as a tie that binds families together or a source of familial discontent; romantic love snugly in hand or disastrously bobbled; the World Series and pick-up games played when young; the game as surreal repository of signs and wonders as well as a stage upon which no-nonsense grit and skill are routinely displayed; matters philosophical and the delight experienced in being one amid a mindlessly happy crowd.

Despite their diversity, what these one hundred poems share is what all good writing manifests: the ability to provoke reflection, recollection, interpretation. Consider Ron Vazzano's "Baseball Haiku":

> Nine men stand waiting
> under storm clouds that gather.
> Someone asks for time.

Time has been called in this game that is subject to no clock, but why and by whom? Does it matter? The nine men are presumably the players on the field, but this is not necessarily so: perhaps only the grouping of nine men outdoors somewhere suggested to the poet a baseball team. Even if they are players, which ones? The catcher might be standing if time has been called, but then where is the batter, and why isn't the number of waiting men at least ten? And why aren't the base coaches and umpires also waiting? Because they are the ones conferring while the players wait? If one imagines a less formal game, then who is being asked to call time? If the nine men include the man at bat, perhaps it is he who has called time, tired of waiting for the pitcher to stop fidgeting. And perhaps the pitcher fidgets because a runner at first (but now we would have at least eleven men) is not standing there like someone waiting for a bus but edging off base: perhaps that is why each line moves a bit further toward the right-hand margin. And perhaps this runner (maybe he's the one calling time?) is causing the pitcher to consider another throw in his direction or to contemplate changing his pitch selection.

But having pondered these matters, we haven't even considered line two yet, those gathering storm clouds. Is time being called by the pitcher because he is ahead after six and the storm will buy him a win, or has the batter called time because his team is hopelessly behind, the game not yet official, and a storm the day's only salvation? Or are we to take those men, those clouds, that desire to stop time less literally, more existentially? Is the poem metaphysically portentous? But if so, of what imminent event beyond a possible storm do these clouds foretell? Does the poem tell us how we all stand helpless before approaching disaster, of how we all sometimes wish to stop time, arrest change? Is this why Vazzano's small vignette arrests us, causes us to linger for how many minutes over a poem that takes perhaps five seconds to read? But even so, why tell this poem in the form of a haiku? Is this game taking place in Japan, or has the form been chosen because the poem is in fact the koan we have found it, for now, to be?

Each of the poems in the pages that follow invites such interrogation, such speculation — some will give the reader quite a workout — for if poetry, like baseball, is serious sport, the reader, too, like the watching fan, must be willing to play. But again: if part of the fun and much of the significance of these poems reside in what we can make of them, the game remains, as Donald Hall has observed, "pure of meaning" (qtd. Hildebidle 181). Or as a character in Woody Allen's 1983 movie *Zelig* says, "I love baseball. You know, it doesn't have to mean anything. It's just very beautiful to watch." Or consider seventeen-year-old Tim Bottorff, speaking in David Cataneo's *Hornsby Hit One over My Head* (a collection of oral histories supplied by everyday fans) of the game's attractiveness in terms of its "meaningless" (and poetic) beauty: "It's the chalk kicking up on a barely fair ball. It's the graceful diving catch. The picture-perfect swing. The rally-killing double play or the flawless execution of the hit and run. You can only explain it with imagery" (261).

If the poems gathered here demonstrate the truth of baseball's encouragement to seductive intellection, they testify as well to the correctness of Allen's and Bottorff's aesthetic appreciation. There is throughout this collection a sensuous attention to sound, to words, and to the skillfully turned phrase: countless metaphors and images that deliver small moments of pure beauty, as when Gailmarie Pahmeier luxuriates in the names of towns — "Idabel, Osceola, or Tonopah" ("Telephone Call") — or Karen Kevorkian listens to her "glove's new lacing creaking / like ship rigging" ("Softball Dreams"), or Quincy Troupe recalls "great black men swinging their lives as bats / at tiny white balls" ("Poem for My Father"). After all, as a truism neatly expressed by the *Chicago Tribune*'s Phil Hersh has it, "baseball is the only game you can see on the radio" because it is a game deeply invested in language and familiar but endlessly evocative sounds: crowd rumble, infield chatter, bat on ball, golden organ oldies, deponing peanut man. (And while we are on the subject of baseball's penchant for inspired uses of language, let's give credit to the players, coaches, announcers, and reporters who have coined those countless metaphors and expressions the game cannot do without — frozen ropes and cans of corn, hittin' shoes and balls with eyes and games that ain't over till they're over.)

We have probably read these poems fifty times, and they continually unfold new layers of beauty and possibility — not all of it exactly mental — much as baseball continues to reveal new mystery and complexity to even its most veteran fans. Indeed, some of the poets gathered here meditate on just this divide: what baseball means or if it does. Perhaps, like Jay Rogoff, when it comes to baseball — or poetry — what we know is "everything but everything." Or perhaps what we know is that these verbal games called poems must strive, no less than baseball itself, to be "perfect and no more meaningless / than anything else" (Karen Zaborowski, "World Series, Game 5").

There is no use attempting to conceal the fact that *Line Drives* is finally a miscellany unified only by the fact that each poem, in one way or another, addresses the subject of baseball. Yet we do believe the book is true to the game's long season and to the lives of those the game engages. Consequently, we have attempted to organize the poems gathered here into five parts, the first four of which sketch a rough trajectory from youth through old age to death; spring to winter; and optimism and joy into moody pessimism and dark brooding. Yet because this is baseball and there is always next year, part five pushes past the defeat inherent in both poetic and athletic striving to allow spring—that season of renewal—to come around again. After all, as Ron McFarland professes at the end of "Why I Love Baseball," "With an old glove . . . and a new baseball, / you could start the whole world over."

Part one, then, begins as the season begins: with spring, youth, optimism, celebration. Yet it is not the case that these poems are without their regrets and grudges any more than spring is without rain or childhood without its disappointment. Thus David Watts's "Little League Tryouts," for instance, arguably offers not only a portrait of nervous ineptitude in the small boys whose "gloves dangle / like suitcases" but a disenchanted comment on these kids' fathers, who "stand / with their well-trained hands / in their pockets," able to pass judgment on children because their own skill, or lack thereof, need not be demonstrated, or perhaps impotently aware of how little they can do to help their kids acquire the skills necessary to feel good about their "play." Or consider Joseph Green's "The Catch," which speaks to the confusion of childhood, of the boy who is probably his team's weakest member (he's been put in right field) as he almost catches a fly ball that for a split second as it "squirts" from his glove hangs "like an insult, so hard and spherical he can't even / understand what everyone around him is shouting."

Part two carries us into summer's lengthening maturity and struggle as hope begins to war with doubt and the cool breezes of childhood give way to the dog days of adulthood. Insights get harder-edged (David Jauss, "How to Hit a Home Run") even if they remain good-natured (Maj Ragain's "Blyleven's Fourth Shutout, June, 1985"; Wyatt Prunty's "Baseball"), and memories begin to circle woes less remediable than not making a team. Thus John C. Pine confesses that even on the day of his father's death baseball could, if momentarily, usurp his consciousness ("Black Ink"), and Yusef Komunyakaa speaks in "Glory" of the recompense baseball provides teenagers married too soon and "Already old men" now "Working knockout shifts daybreak / To sunset six days a week. . . ." Yet if adulthood brings its defeats and damage, if the poems of part two are perhaps reluctant to proffer unqualified praise of one's baseball days, summer is also a good time for lust and love (Jay Rogoff's "Aesthetics," Rebecca J. Finch's "Ode to Apple Pie"), for sunstruck reflections on how baseball helps make and explain a life. And as Rina Ferrarelli's "Crowd at the Stadium," Andrew Hudgins's "In the Red Seats," and Jim Daniels's "Polish-American Night, Tiger Stadium" suggest, there is still time for games where the losses belong mostly to others. As part two closes, we edge into the past as the best we are likely to know begins the slow process of becoming memory.

"Show me a hero," wrote F. Scott Fitzgerald, "and I'll write you a tragedy" (qtd. in Schinto xvi). Consequently, in parts three and four, our poems grow autumnal, then downright wintry, as they meditate upon lost youth, lost fathers, lost time, lost hopes, lost love while holding fast to whatever lessons have been learned, to whatever consolation age and wisdom might manage to redeem. This shift to a more somber mood is signaled in part three's opening poem with its surreal description of a ball game "called on / account of / fear" (Richard Brautigan, "A Baseball Game") and in the David Starkey poem that follows in which pears "Hard / as baseballs" fall to the ground and, soaked by rain, swell "to softball size," then "burst / into foul decay" ("September Pears").

In these two sections can be found poems of increasing disillusionment with the game and with the world for which baseball is microcosm; poems of careers ending (Dan Quisenberry's "Baseball Cards," Tony Cosier's "Southpaw"); of historical loss and shame (Constantine von Hoffman's "Geronimo at Short," Dale Ritterbusch's "World Series, 1968, Southeast Asia"); of philosophical mulling (Michael Blumenthal's "Night Baseball," Laurence Goldstein's "Is Reality One or Many?") and cynical indictment (Mark W. Schraf's "Question and Answer"). Poems of old age and death — Jim Daniels's "Play by Play," Michelle Jones's "My Father, on the Day He Died," Charles Bukowski's "Betting on the Muse" — percolate through these often agonizing sections of dream and nightmare, of struggles recollected or foreseen. Part four ends with Philip Dacey's imagining of an end to all baseball seasons ("America Without Baseball") and George Looney's attempt to find the means of escaping the sin and loss forever threatening to overwhelm us, an effort that like a nervous batter would erase the lines (between the sacred and the profane, between baseball and the rest of our lives) that box us in and keep us from where we want to be.

If many of the poems in parts three and four manage to salvage from decline such virtues as hope, wisdom, courage, or an appreciation for what has been and for what remains, part five rewards such salvation. Spring gradually returns, although its praise and promise are now tempered by the knowledge that, as Robert Gibb puts it, in our "realm of decline" we never know "how long / [Our] momentary days will continue / To fill with such splendid ease" ("Listening to the Ballgame"). Or as Joel Lewis would have it, despite the realization that all of our accomplishments are "physical graffiti / in a world of samsara," one need never lose "the plain / joy of fielding a pop-up by the dusty / lip of the dugout" or the beauty of those "grey chrysanthemums / that base runners create / as they slide into home plate . . . " ("A Dharma Talk by Johnny Roseboro, Boulder, Colorado, March 23, 1983").

What baseball gives us, these closing poems suggest, is the desire always to be "staggered with joy" (Keith Eisner, "Shall I Compare Thee to a Triple Play?"), mere games that "make the weeks go by so personal, / so hand in glove" (Linda Gregerson, "Line Drive Caught by the Grace of God"). And we can feel this hand-in-glove joy, Richard Behm's magisterial "Looking for the Baseball" argues, because however lost or misplaced our paradise, however much even the birds sing us "songs of desolation and terror" as we slip-slide into disbelief, "in an obvious place," and "right where it should be," we will always find baseball.

We hope you feel the same way.

Notes

1. Or perhaps it is the fate of any would-be serious art that takes as its ostensible subject so trivial a thing as a homespun game. It was, after all, John Smith who complained in 1607 of the Jamestown settlers that "4 hours each day was spent in works, the rest in pastimes and merry exercise," and William Penn who in *No Cross, No Crown* (1669) averred that men must not "eat, drink, play, game and sport away their irrevocable precious time" (qtd. in Gorn and Goldstein 19, 37).

2. Baseball poetry routinely appears in the pages of *Aethlon: The Journal of Sport Literature* (formerly *Arete: The Journal of Sport Literature*), *Elysian Fields Quarterly* (formerly the *Minneapolis Review of Baseball*), *Fan Magazine*, and *Spitball: The Literary Baseball Magazine*.

3. Of the many anthologies that have appeared over the years devoted to the literature of baseball, without doubt the best book devoted exclusively to baseball poetry is Don Johnson's *Hummers, Knucklers, and Slow Curves*. Of books containing prose and poetry, the best are *Baseball Diamonds* and *Baseball I Gave You All the Best Years of My Life*, both edited by Kevin Kerrane and Richard Grossinger, and *Diamonds Are a Girl's Best Friend*, edited by Elinor Nauen. Also of interest are Grossinger's *The Temple of Baseball*, Tom Tolnay's recent *Baseball and the Lyrical Life*, and *The Mudville Diaries*, edited by Mike Schacht. Grossinger's *The Dreamlife of Johnny Baseball* is also worth a look although it contains only thirteen poems.

Of less interest simply because they contain fewer poems (and often frequently reprinted poems as well as early baseball verse) are the Fireside books of baseball edited by Charles Einstein (here can be found classic poems by Grantland Rice, Ernest Thayer, Marianne Moore, Kenneth Patchen, Robert Francis, John Updike, and others). *Diamonds Are Forever: Artists and Writers on Baseball*, edited by Peter H. Gordon with the assistance of Sydney Waller and Paul Weinman, also contains a large handful (seventeen, to be exact) of worthwhile if often familiar poems.

Anthologies devoted to sport in general that contain a number of baseball poems include Tom Dodge's excellent *A Literature of Sports*, Emilie Buchwald and Ruth Roston's *This Sporting Life*, R. R. Knudson and May Swenson's *American Sports Poems*, and Noah Blaustein's recent *Motion: American Sports Poems*.

4. It was for such reasons that we omitted such otherwise fine poems as Hugh Abernathy's "American Legends in Paris," which offers a reply to Gregory Corso's classic "Dream of a Baseball Star," and Michael Gilmartin's "e. e. cummings/pete rose goings," which rewrites Cummings's popular "Buffalo Bill's / defunct."

5. One minor exception to this rule is that we have let stand Charles Bukowski's misspelling of Jimmie Foxx's name.

6. Recent long poems and sequences of particular note include Kevin Bezner's twenty-six-section prose-poem, "The Tools of Ignorance"; George Bowering's series, "Yards"; Bob Chicoine's "The Wrecking of Old Comiskey"; Donald Hall's "Baseball" (including "Extra Innings"); Kenneth Koch's "Ko, or a Season on Earth"; Daniel Martin's "The Grey Arc of a Local Hero"; and Robert Joe Stout's chapbook-length series *They Still Play Baseball the Old Way*. Similarly, we felt that Paul Weinman's gritty, unsentimental hardball poems — as collected in *Hardball Ain't All Bucolic* and *He Swings a Straight Stick* — really worked best as contributory parts of a cumulative effect.

Works Cited

Abernathy, Hugh, Jr. "American Legends in Paris." *Minneapolis Review of Baseball* 9.3 (1990): 5.

Barzun, Jacques. *God's Country and Mine: A Declaration of Love Spiced with a Few Harsh Words.* Boston: Atlantic Monthly-Little, 1954.

Bezner, Kevin. "The Tools of Ignorance." *The Tools of Ignorance.* Cincinnati: Cincinnati Writers' Project, 1997. 3–10.

Blaustein, Noah, ed. *Motion: American Sports Poems.* Iowa City: U of Iowa P, 2001.

Bowering, George. "Yards." *Urban Snow.* Vancouver: Talonbooks, 1991. 71–92.

Buchwald, Emilie, and Ruth Roston, eds. *This Sporting Life: Poems about Sports and Games.* Minneapolis: Milkweed, 1987.

Cataneo, David. *Hornsby Hit One over My Head: A Fan's Oral History of Baseball.* San Diego: Harcourt, 1997.

Chicoine, Bob. "The Wrecking of Old Comiskey." *Spitball* 44 (1993): 36–59.

Corso, Gregory. "Dream of a Baseball Star." *The Happy Birthday of Death.* New York: New Directions, 1960. 45.

Cummings, E. E. "Buffalo Bill's." *Complete Poems 1913–1962.* New York: Harcourt, 1972. 69.

Dodge, Tom, ed. *A Literature of Sports.* Lexington, MA: Heath, 1980.

Einstein, Charles, ed. *The Fireside Book of Baseball.* New York: Simon, 1956. (Released in 1987 with new contents under the same title as "4th ed.")

———. *The New Baseball Reader: More Favorites from the Fireside Books of Baseball.* New York: Viking, 1991.

———. *The Second Fireside Book of Baseball.* New York: Simon, 1958.

———. *The Third Fireside Book of Baseball.* New York: Simon, 1968.

Gilmartin, Michael. "e. e. cummings/pete rose goings." *Elysian Fields Quarterly* 12.4 (1994): 30.

Gordon, Peter H., with Sydney Waller and Paul Weinman, eds. *Diamonds Are Forever: Artists and Writers on Baseball.* San Francisco: Chronicle, 1987.

Gorn, Elliot J., and Warren Goldstein. *A Brief History of American Sports.* New York: Hill and Wang, 1993.

Grossinger, Richard, ed. *The Dreamlife of Johnny Baseball.* Berkeley: North Atlantic, 1987.

———. *The Temple of Baseball.* Berkeley: North Atlantic, 1985.

Hall, Donald. "Baseball" (including "Extra Innings"). *The Museum of Clear Ideas.* New York: Ticknor, 1993. 13–39, 103–15.

Hersh, Phil. "Baseball Is a Dream that Can't Go Away." *Chicago Tribune* 11 Aug. 1985, late ed.: sports sec. 1.

Hildebidle, John. "Baseball and the Life of the Mind." *New England Review/Bread Loaf Quarterly* 7 (1984). Rpt. in *Baseball and the Game of Ideas: Essays for the Serious Fan.* Ed. Peter Bjarkman. Delhi, NY: Birch Brook P, 179–93.

Johnson, Don, ed. *Hummers, Knucklers, and Slow Curves: Contemporary Baseball Poems*. Urbana: U of Illinois P, 1991.

Kerrane, Kevin, and Richard Grossinger, eds. *Baseball Diamonds: Tales, Traces, Visions, and Voodoo from a Native American Rite*. Garden City: Anchor, 1980.

———. *Baseball I Gave You All the Best Years of My Life*. Oakland: North Atlantic, 1977.

Knudson, R. R., and May Swenson, eds. *American Sports Poems*. New York: Orchard, 1988.

Koch, Kenneth. "Ko, or a Season on Earth." *Seasons on Earth*. New York: Penguin, 1987. 21–131.

Littlefield, Bill. "Ballpark Rhapsody." *Boston Magazine* May 1990: 64, 71.

Martin, Daniel. "The Grey Arc of a Local Hero." *Spitball* 29 (1989): 2–52.

Matthews, William. "Dull Subjects." *New England Review/Bread Loaf Quarterly* 8 (1985): 142–52.

Nauen, Elinor, ed. *Diamonds Are a Girl's Best Friend: Women Writers on Baseball*. Boston: Faber, 1994.

Schacht, Mike, ed. *The Mudville Diaries: A Book of Baseball Memories*. New York: Avon, 1996.

Schinto, Jeanne. Introduction. *Show Me a Hero: Great Contemporary Stories about Sports*. Ed. Jeanne Schinto. New York: Persea, 1995. xiii–xviii.

Stout, Robert Joe. *They Still Play Baseball the Old Way*. Fox River Grove, IL: White Eagle Coffee Store P, 1994.

Tolnay, Tom, ed. *Baseball and the Lyrical Life: Poetry and Diamond Dust*. Delhi, NY: Birch Brook P, 1999.

Weinman, Paul. *Baseball Ain't All Bucolic*. Richford, VT: Samisdat, 1986.

———. *He Swings a Straight Stick*. Richford, VT: Samisdat, 1985.

ONE

RICHARD BEHM

The Origin and Purpose of Baseball

It began on the veldt
when snakes were common,
and a woman
searching for food
saw the moon and thought
it was an egg
that her children might eat.
She plucked it from the sky
and took it home.

Her children kicked
and clawed and fought
and called each other names,
until the woman and the moon
gave order to their games,
rules based on the rhythms
of the sea, birth, the geometry
of hope, the mysteries
of nines and threes.

So in the last of the ninth,
bases loaded, two out,
the pitcher hitches his belt,
winds, kicks a leg
at heaven,
and the egg spins toward the plate
where a child with a stick
that his mother used to batter snakes
waits.

When the child connects
it is the moon that rises,
that long line drive
into tomorrow, the crowd
thundering to its feet,
the ball sailing out of the park,
climbing again the night,
hanging there, cold, perfect,
out of reach.

Spring Fever

Last Sunday in February.
Neighbors lean on warm cars.
Snow pulls away from the grass.

At the corner variety store
kids huddle out front,
hustle off, scattering
baseball card wrappers
colorful as April tulips.

Stealing Home

arriving in a strange city
        ideally the play is tried with two outs
where I was once a child
        and less than two strikes on the batter
I meet the first crocuses of spring
        left-handers using full windups
fierce salvos of color fired through
        provide the best chance
pale ironies of melting snow
        you will need about four seconds
as I imagine the flowers unfolding
        to cover the distance
faces from childhood
        from the leadoff to headlong slide
come unexpectedly to mind

ELINOR NAUEN

Spring Training
for Becky

Full speed ahead! in fact it
is here & alas I am there that is to say
I am here & the Yankees are in Florida
where the green & blue are extreme & particular
and a blaze of sun anoints the heroes
of a ruthless nostalgic crowd
of dreamers. Dave Winfield is wearing
wire-rim glasses & describing his education.
I am in right field with a catcher's mitt
playing for the Twins in pinstripes &
self-consciousness. The newspapers make very little
of a woman making the team. Nor do they think it strange
I'm as old as Dave. Dave does though.
Your unlined skin! he marvels. Your jet-black hair!
And an autodidact to boot.
Boot an easy fly, I mutter nervously.
Dave looks stern. What do you call an Irishman
who's been buried for 50 years?
Billy Martin? I suggest.
Pete! he laughs, I laugh, we all laugh.
It is spring & it is baseball & the Yankees
are "guaranteed a world championship"
& life is as simple as a slow roll foul
down the first-base line.

DAVID WATTS

Little League Tryouts

Tiny fellows
line up
with cardboard numbers
pinned to their backs
like kites
dancing before the moment
of flight.

Their gloves dangle
like suitcases,
the shoulders
slant, they hurl
themselves in front
of grounders, they
swing the bat, the bat
swings them, they swarm
under fly balls
like minnows.

And the fathers stand
with their well-trained hands
in their pockets.

JOSEPH GREEN

The Catch

Under a high fly ball to right
a boy runs in, calling *I got it,*
then changes his mind and backpedals.
No place anywhere is lonelier than right field now.

Half the parents in the bleachers pray for him
to get this one; then the other half give thanks
for what happens: the ball squirts up from the web
of his glove, a trout leaping out of water's grip,

and in the suspended moment before it falls
back into gravity's lap, it hangs over the boy
like an insult, so hard and spherical that he can't even
understand what everyone around him is shouting.

J. CAITLIN OAKES

Baseball

A ball rips through the sky
and into the open window of a house
where a boy forgets what a woman taught him
yesterday. They've been doing right angles
and triangles for days and he can't quite get
what would be under her shirt
if it did come off. The baseball rolls
under the downstairs couch
and no one knows it's there for weeks.

Outside, eight boys shine up another ball.
It's pitched, then smacked,
and another hole is torn in the shape
of a high-spun arch. A woman's song
rushes into the tunnel the ball has made
and fills the space that's left behind.
Her song, every whole dusky note, lands
in the mitt of a twelve year old
and his hands are shocked around it.

It quivers. It might as well be shining
and he leaps, making a perfect throw
to head off the runner at third and,
yes! The ball's path fills a young man's
song or lost duet. All afternoon
and into evening, balls tear the air
from space and their trails
are filled with song. It's late
and no one's tired.

The boy who must be tutored
is downstairs now. He walks through the path

where the ball had passed
and where the song that follows lingers.
A lovely weight enters each palm.
The pressure is warm and firm
in his hands. His father reads to him
from some old book but the boy thinks circles,
then full spheres.

The Player
for Gabriel

Beyond the window, caught in the yard's arena,
my son is batting a thousand.
Throw, hit, slide: he does it all.
With solitary grace, flexed and unaware,
he gathers the world around him
in a cloak of intent:
making order from the chaos of the day,
calming a confusion of mysteries
with the power of threes.

In a silent moment I sweep clean my soul
and fling its burdens over him like a net.
How much better he could bear them!
Perhaps it is the window between us;
they do not stick; he is charmed.
I draw them back, dew-soaked, heavier than before.

Throw, hit, slide: the fan goes wild
with love, with longing,
wanting to be both the player and the wise one
who sits apart in the stands and prays.

1947

Once
boys played baseball
without adults,
even on Saturdays.
Fathers,
thinking more of sons then,
knew one was always out
on a close play
and did not interfere.
And sometimes,
after supper
in the hot hushed evenings of July
the fathers would come out
like shy children
in their tee-shirts and dress pants,
and they would hit
huge parabolic drives
that cracked through the dry sycamores
many yards away,
and run the short base paths
in their thin dark socks
that would never come clean
for work again,
and pause in their great glee
to breathe hard and light cigarettes.
We relayed those long balls
by brigades
until it was too dark to see;

then we all walked home
under a full moon
nestled in the sky
like a new baseball
in a worn mitt.

WESLEY MCNAIR

The Retarded Children Play Baseball

Never mind the coaches who try
to teach them the game,
and think of the pleasure

of the large-faced boy
on second who raises hand and glove
straight up making the precise

shape of a ball, even though
the ball's now over
the outfield. And think of the left

and right fielders going deeper
just to watch its roundness
materialize out of the sky

and drop at their feet. Both teams
are so in love with this moment
when the bat makes the ball jump

or fly that when it happens
everybody shouts, and the girl
with slanted eyes on first base

leaps off to let the batter by.
Forget the coaches shouting back
about the way the game is played

and consider the game
they're already playing, or playing
perhaps elsewhere on some other field,

like the shortstop, who stands transfixed
all through the action, staring
at what appears to be nothing.

BETH ANN FENNELLY

Asked for a Happy Memory of Her Father, She Remembers Wrigley Field

His drinking was different in sunshine,
as if it couldn't be bad. Sudden, manic,
he swung into a laugh, bought me
two ice creams, said *One for each hand.*

Half the hot game I licked Good Humor
running down wrists. My bird mother earlier,
packing my pockets with sun block,
had hopped her warning: *Be careful.*

So, pinned between his knees, I held
his Old Style in both hands
while he streaked the cream on my cheeks
and slurred, *My little Indian princess.*

Home run: the hairy necks of men in front
jumped up, thighs torn from gummy green bleachers
to join the violent scramble. Father
held me close and said, *Be careful,*

be careful. But why should I be full of care
with his thick arms circling my shoulders,
with a high smiling sun, like a home run,
in the upper right-hand corner of the sky?

LINDSAY KNOWLTON

Sweet Spot

Peering through ridiculously large glasses
that pinch his ears, the boy
grips his father's hand
as another player ambles out to the mound,
scuffs the dust, holds trigger-cocked still
like a trout idling,
then spins around for the pitch.

Big-league — big time, but it can be a long night
under the lights,
and even with his felt pennant and glossy souvenirs,
why the fuss?
Nothing seems to happen; neither team scores.
Men are walked, men struck out,
and like so many Dixie cups littering the field,
the innings pile up. By the bottom of the seventh,
fidgety and stiff, the boy wants someone
to be hurt, or else to go home.

But maybe he'll learn, by staying, the shame
of the failed connection, the proportion
of strikes and fouls, and how often, like wrong words,
pain must be taken back — first along
the shocked fibers of the swung bat, then
up into the body's shaft until the next time on deck,
the next brief try. So when at the top of the eighth,
with one man on and hope of any break stalled
in the air, the slammer comes hard,

the boy feels the whack, feels something like a hot
white brick fly out of his chest,
and less dumb now to odds,
he stomps on the bleachers and swallows
hard before he too lets out a roar
along with the whole manic crowd, now pennant-crazed
—now giddy on its feet.

EDWIN ROMOND

Something I Could Tell You about Love

The soft smack of pitches from my father
who's never cared for baseball, and never asks
about my Yankees. He doesn't want a glove,
just lets my hardball disappear into his hands
already sore from steering his truck without AC
or radio through the decay of Newark and Elizabeth.
My father, whose shirt's glued with sweat,
knows drums and crates must be loaded tonight
but still stands and throws to me across the hood
of his '53 Ford sagging with freight he'll have to carry
tomorrow into hardware stores and dentists' offices.
Tonight I pound the second-hand glove he bought me
and watch his face grow dim in the dark of our yard,
then the white ball from his hands into the August heat.
I'm playing catch with my father, who's never liked baseball,
who nods when I ask for five minutes more.

To Fungo the Torn Ones

My father would fungo the torn ones into orbit,
a rising, zippered sound, heading beyond
the outfield, across New Virginia Road,
into the tall weeds,

all out of proportion to this world,
too fast, too high, then gone.

We were transfixed,
each seeking the moment of reappearance,
something-out-of-nothingness,
the long descent gathering speed,
the sudden thud into earth.

* * *

There was a dog in space
in a capsule the size
of a washing machine.

He looked down on us.

There were line drives and missiles,
hydrants and fire hoses.
Poets died, monks
burned in the streets.

When four or five had plummeted,
hard-nosed, into the Queen Anne's Lace,
and there were only good balls left,

we'd go for ice cream and return to our houses,
to our sidewalks and televisions,
hands sticky as blood, a dog
barking somewhere above us.

The Baseball Boys of 1964

Bobby Jo loved my sister Sarah
deep in the woods behind our house
and I pretended not to notice
he was whiter than most of the other boys.
With red hair he was flaming.
It's a wonder they didn't set the woods afire.

But that's another story. This is a baseball story
about Bobby Richardson and Clete Boyer
playing second and third for the Yankees.
Whitey Ford was still on the mound humming
fast balls and side arm sliders to Elston Howard
catching hell for being one of the first
coloreds behind the plate

glass window Bobby Jo broke
with one of the longest home runs I've ever seen.
Roberto Clemente was playing center
for the Pirates and Sandy Koufax was hurling
left-handed hooks
I don't think anyone could hit

the beat-up baseball we played with
that summer I was 14 and Bobby Jo was 15 and a half.
Some days would catch us stealing honey buns
from Mr. Kye Howard's store while
Maury Wills, "The Saturday Afternoon Blur,"
was stealing bases for the Dodgers.

Hank Aaron was always in the batter's box
trying to knock Milwaukee one run ahead
of San Francisco's Willie Mays playing in the center
of Candlestick Park chasing down every fly ball.

It was a time of shoe boxes and baseball cards
in the pockets of school yard boys huddled
around Mr. McGee, listening to the World Series
on a portable radio that kept going in and out

looking for another shoe box big enough to hold
my cards. "Name a player and I will tell you
his lifetime batting average or his ERA."
Roger Maris was hitting more home runs
but big-stick Mickey Mantle was batting "clean up

your room," Grandma would say
every Saturday morning before I went to the field
to meet Bobby Jo.
Hampstead was a town where everyone was poor.
I had a ball and Bobby Jo had a Louisville Slugger
on his shoulder waiting for me
to throw that one change-up that would change
the direction of the wind as it sailed
across the fence

that caged Bobby Jo's feelings of being
the only white boy in town that wasn't afraid
to call me his best buddy.

Perhaps the others were afraid because
none of them could play every position like me
and Bobby Jo behind the plate catching fast balls
without a mask, daring anyone to steal second.

But I stole second like I stole Mr. Kye Howard's sweet cakes
because I was quicker than the deer we hunted
that fall on Mr. Jack Lea's property.

Chicago had Ernie Banks and Billy Williams
but they couldn't ever win an even chance
to play 7 games in the fields of my childhood
overgrown with weeds, covered with holes.
We knew exactly where every hole was
even when we were chasing fly balls.

Bobby Jo's father, I don't think he ever said a word
but his mother used to get real mad
every time I came in the front door
when the Milwaukee Braves were playing
and Eddie Matthews was knocking home runs.

That was my favorite team. I don't know why.
Perhaps because my brother Lee gave me a cap
with a big M on it the year he died.
It was a small funeral where no one cried.
Bobby Jo's mother wouldn't let him go.

It's been almost 20 years now
and I miss what I think he could have been.
He wasn't much good at baseball
but he had a head for facts and figures.
Maybe he could have been a manager
like old Casey Stengel. I don't know

what difference that little fish house town has made in my life
of roaming deer and running bases
that sometimes seemed spaced out just a bit farther
because I was the only colored boy around.

Some days I tried to talk to Bobby Jo
about life but he didn't care about anything
but the seams of a baseball. I guess
his hair was just a little too red
to measure the distance from home plate
to second base and back or what it would take
for me to play centerfield
on the only church team in town.

LOUISE GRIECO

It Ain't Over . . .

Baseball is something
like love. There's an elegance
about it—a fine tension.

Fielders pluck comets
from thin and glorious air.
Pitchers make solid spheres
disappear. And batters smash meteors
with matchsticks.

But fielders also topple
over fences, sprawl empty-handed
in the dust. Pitchers throw wild.
And batters sometimes tilt
at windmills.

Yet they lean in—watch—wait.
They risk looking foolish
in order to be brilliant.

M. L. LIEBLER

Instant Out

The infield-fly rule
Beautiful zen thought cut in
A diamond of lawn

Baseball Fields Seen from the Air

In the absolute panic of landing,
these are the best of all possible signs.

Their sandy fans unfold below.
Home is the hub of that sweet green breeze.

Pie in the sky, pie of the irrefutable 'earth!
Each field is a thick delicious slice.

A little-league park that's a red-clay scar,
a minor-league field with mange,

a major-league stadium's emerald diamond
set in a golden scallop shell—

they all broadcast the same welcome message,
V for victory, peace be with you.

What crop could grow in such peculiar fields?
What silt-rich rivers left such deltas?

The plane's loud shadow haunts the waiting game.
There's a sudden sound that will release us.

Each field is a clock where time has stopped,
fair hands frozen at the quarter hour.

DAVID BAKER

Cardinals in Spring
after Whitman

1.
Tens of thousands on the wing, perennial in April
— think how pure we are now, in retrospect —
tens of thousands in our red caps wheeling down
from Davenport, St. Charles, from Boonville by the river,
from our populous sadnesses driven,

from our seedy backyards driven,
from the bullies and yahoos and doddering folk
of our neighborhoods driven to reclaim
our rightful seats, St. Louis, Busch Stadium, 1968, the same
as '67, as '66, and the season's first pitch.

2.
I don't deny this whole thing
is designed to celebrate our most common desires:
it's spring, we want to win, things grow, we feel
inside ourselves the power of something so immense and primitive
it spreads out unchecked, ritual. *Redbirds!* We sing

as they take the field, uniforms like shiny hieroglyphs,
and scatter across the Astroturf, a sun-lit plain of green stuff
hopefully forever so green, our latest synthesis
of industry, imagination, and the persistent pastoral archetype.
We're all here, never more perfect than now . . .

3.
Brock of the basepath, never more perfect than now,
Javier of the hopping grounder, never quicker,
Flood in his field, and Shannon, and Maxvill at short,
McCarver-in-a-crouch, and suddenly Gibby
whipping his warm-ups in from the natural dirt of the mound . . .

Mom with her bag of fried chicken, Dad with his cooler,
Dad with his scorecard and program, my brother next to him,
Uncle Buster crowding down who yesterday flipped
a knuckler behind his back so powerfully
it arched through an upstairs window . . . never more perfect than now.

4.
What is it? I wonder, and Buster brings his arm up to me.
We're all in our red, at last in our row,
Green Level, Section 6, and everywhere the fragrance
of hotdogs and beer, the press of bodies, the voices of thousands
like us chattering, communally wild. *O what is it?*

and now Buster opens his hand, his pure-white present,
and everyone is applauding in one body,
and the sun flames down, and the pressbox glasses over, adazzle,
and I am jumping; and now I think it must be
the icy chiseled heart of winter melting in his outheld palm,

5.
it is that incredible; and now I think
it is the pure/seamy duality of rewritten lives crossing, forever
stitched in red, the yin and yang of postmodern expression,
and nothing less; and now the hatching egg of hope;
and he looks at me; and now I think it is

an antique opaque eyeball, a foggy crystal ball
through which even cliché transcends itself and so signifies
our inarticulate, collective excitement that nothing
in particular, always already, is happening with sensational urgency
. . . and now he's giving it to me . . .

6.
But how can I know that? How can I say all that?
How can I be 13 and 33 at once, cursed and blessed, crying
with all the fever and joy of the stupid
who know the truth and can't speak it, yet speaking, *here* . . .
    he's giving it to me, and I hold it, *a baseball*

signed by the entire team! I know it: *This is mine*
to love! the whole weighty globe of it, the tens of thousands
in our companionable nest, even the other team loping afield . . .
whoever they are, my own affections having blurred,
for a moment, all the individual images . . .

7.
When we stand, as we must, when the silence
and fragrant calm settle over us all, as surely they must,
and the caps come off and our hands flutter up
to our felt hearts, when we begin to sing
in a voice so singular it redoubles, echoing off the sky,

we stretch ourselves proud and pulsing, and the music,
like an organic truth, throbs through our veins and temples,
and over the land of the free, *over the vendors and hawkers,*
over athletes and umps, the fireworks blossom
into smoke-puffs and thunder like the storms of creation.

8.
The moment before its beak breaks through the tender shell,
doesn't the fledgling struggle for its whole species,
doesn't its becoming, at that moment, signify freedom and flight,
doesn't longing belong to the family of hope?
And when we sit back trembling and rapt with anticipation,

don't we personify our teeming, human compulsions?
Yet how can we say these things in real life?
All in the space of a moment, between silence and screaming,
between breath and breath, suspended in the nether-sphere
of original joy, aren't we, in each other, renewed?

9.
O thousands of us, tens of thousands with our souvenirs
and our statistics committed to memory where all things
change for the better, we are the bodies of a single desire.

And now Gibby, across the semi-precious green diamond,
across the dumbstruck years, stares in for his sign, turns,

and hurtles the first pitch, winging it outward,
and we are leaping up, mouthing our first word O,
and the ball leaves his whipped arm, and hangs there, for us all,
for this moment, this beginning, where I see it still,
all of us, O! never more perfect than now.

Stop Action

Slowly as in an underwater dance
the shortstop dips to take the ball
on a low hop, swings back his arm, balancing
without thought, all muscles intending
the diagonal to the first baseman's glove.

As the ball leaves his hand, the action stops —
and, watching, we feel a curious poignancy,
a catch in the throat. It is not this play
only. Whenever the sweet drive is stopped
and held, our breath wells up like the rush

of sadness or longing we sometimes feel
without remembering the cause of it.
The absolute moment gathers the surge
and muscle of the past, complete,
yet hurling itself forward — arrested
here between its birth and perishing.

TWO

DAVID JAUSS

How to Hit a Home Run

1.

Get yourself a bat with a grain so thin you need glasses to read it (this is a sign the wood is under greater pressure than you'll ever be) and name it after your secret lover, the one who comes to you only in dreams. (If you don't know her name, don't expect anything but singles all your life.)

2.

Practice your swing while reciting the names of everyone who ever betrayed you. Swing a little harder each time until you reach your own name. Then swing with everything you've got.

3.

Accept that there is always some waver in the foul lines. And pay the lines, faulty though they be, the homage due them: always step over them when you take or leave the field. (Remember what stepping on a mere sidewalk crack can do.)

4.

The batter's box is a different story: show these lines no respect. Kick dirt on them, scratch them out with your cleats. Allow no restrictions here, where you must shape your own home.

5.

Know the umpire wears more than one mask. Distrust the one that looks like skin. And know, too, he will call anything over the black edges of this stark place you call home a strike, and say it's in the rulebook. And it is. So thank him each time he calls a strike. But dispute each ball.

6.
Before the pitcher takes the sign, think of all the girls you never got to first base with. Then imagine three strikes whistling past while the bat sleeps on your shoulder. Rub dirt on your hands in penance.

7.
Never forget the pitcher holds death by his fingertips. It can get away from him at any time. The scorer calls this a wild pitch, but you know better: nothing is more civilized than the pitch that makes you hit the dirt, where you belong. So do not insist on the false dignity of two feet firmly planted. Be ready to fall.

8.
Scorn the pitcher's magic act. Granted: he can make the ball vanish then reappear in the catcher's mitt. But you're the one waving the biggest magic wand of them all.

9.
Think of all the reasons you should never have been born. Then wait for the dark one down the middle and lose yourself in it so that when you meet it square you're ready to begin the long run back to where you must begin again.

Blyleven's Fourth Shutout, June, 1985

The Cleveland Indians are up
two to nothing, bottom of the eighth.
The Dutchman has his curveball tonight.
I can hear it snap off,
even on the car radio.
I am sitting half drunk
in the driveway, listening to the game
in my pinstripes.
The women and children have gone to the house.
The new summer darkness counts the outs.

Somebody should drop
a cold mountain on the car
right now, bury me
in the driveway with the shutout.
I'd live a day or two
till the battery, the beer or
the game ran out.

My grown son Sean
is a second baseman
in the slow-pitch league.
He would be the one
to climb the mountain of my grave
and live with the puzzle
of the short series
playing against
the soles of his shoes.

Baseball

About the time I got my first-baseman's mitt
I heard that Dizzy Dean was sacked
Because he made a dirty comment
Over the air. Camera zoomed and locked
On a young couple kissing, something slipped
With Dizzy, who then made the call:
"He kisses her on every strike,
And she kisses him on the balls."

In a century banked with guilt and doubt
Sometimes the telling moments come
As inadvertently as Dizzy's joke,
Like Hitler's code before Coventry was bombed,
Or Valéry's remark about Descartes:
"I sometimes think, therefore I sometimes am."

Black Ink

1.

As teenagers
We went skating on Black Ink
In the estates section of Roslyn;
The winter sun shone dimly
Through tangled willow trees.
On the way home
We passed Christopher Morley's house
And circled warily around
His imposing presence.
A remote, aging celebrity,
He wrote a best seller called *Kitty Foyle*
In the middle of the Great Depression.

2.

Joe Raddigan's old man was out of work;
An ex–railroad man, he brooded
From his front porch and occasionally
Took a mild interest in our baseball games
In the empty lot behind the house.
My father was more fortunate;
A pier superintendent, he worked
Sixty or seventy hours a week
On the Brooklyn docks loading steel
Bound for San Francisco and the Golden Gate,
Then under construction.

3.

He died of a heart attack
On a beautiful spring day in 1941,
While sitting peacefully in his best Sunday clothes
In the back yard of our rented house on Glenwood Road.

While I was waiting for the ambulance,
Some kids I knew passed in a car
And asked me if I were going over to the school
To play baseball. Stupidly,
I told them I'd be over later.

PETER MEINKE

A Dream of Third Base

Night after night, frozen at third base,
I lean toward a throw I know I must catch
but don't stretch far enough:
the ball sails off, the runner
slides snarling at my feet. Then
right away and once again—
bare-handed as before the fall—
perched on third in the starless air,
the runner's shadow darkening the path,
I wait for that accursed ball.

I think I'm afraid it will hurt:
the ball is coming too fast;
the catcher with his thick wrists
has reared and fired like a loaded gun—
or the snake-armed shortstop whose lidless eyes . . .

Surely baseball stands for something else—
I haven't been a fan
since the Dodgers abandoned Ebbetts Field;
we used to go on Sunday, my dad and I,
breaking the Fourth Commandment . . .

The field is Paradise, then, all green and new:
we're young and quick of foot, our cries
rise in the springtime air.

And then we're given a ball.
And then we're given a bat.
Who are those men in black?

It starts hurting after that.

But why, for me, *that* place? "*Nel mezzo
del cammin di nostra vita*, I awoke on third base."

Dante would have loved baseball, all those nines
and threes (even the stands stand
for something else: howling gluttons
stuff hot dogs down their throats).
I crouch at third, the corner eternally hot,
with Eros on the mound and Thanatos at bat—
while the citizens stomp their feet,
waving doleful undershirts—
remembering the thick wrists of my father,
the infield's skin, the ball with its stitches turning;
drafted into this dream
by some archetypal team
my cleats dig into the dirt,
my hand already burning:
guilty, small, and hurt.

Glory

Most were married teenagers
Working knockout shifts daybreak
To sunset six days a week—
Already old men playing ball
In a field between a row of shotgun houses
& the Magazine Lumber Company.
They were all Jackie Robinson
& Willie Mays, a touch of
Josh Gibson & Satchel Paige
In each stance & swing, a promise
Like a hesitation pitch always
At the edge of their lives,
Arms sharp as rifles.
The Sunday afternoon heat
Flared like thin flowered skirts
As children & wives cheered.
The men were like cats
Running backwards to snag
Pop-ups & high-flies off
Fences, stealing each other's glory.
The old deacons & raconteurs
Who umpired made an *Out* or *Safe*
Into a song & dance routine.
Runners hit the dirt
& slid into homeplate,
Cleats catching light,
As they conjured escapes, outfoxing
Double plays. In the few seconds
It took a man to eye a woman
Upon the makeshift bleachers,

A stolen base or homerun
Would help another man
Survive the new week.

Aesthetics

Invisible in her dark lectures
    I'd see my prof's eyes
        shine like the blues
in saintly Venetian pictures,

but it wasn't Survey where I fell—
    she wore a Yankees cap,
        halter top,
and cargo shorts, playing softball,

a faculty-family pickup game.
    Crouching behind the plate,
        "Choke the bat,"
she told her son, on the other team,

who scrunched down lower at the plate,
    held the bat at the knob,
        swung at a lob,
and popped out into his mom's mitt.

When she sprang up I watched the long
    line from behind her knee
        up her thigh
(to study its sculpture with my tongue!),

and when she batted she poked
    a soft liner past first
        and burst
out laughing as she joked

with my English prof, who said, "Some
    mother *you* are." Quick laugh.
      Then she took off
on a deep double and came home.

You can't define it and not say "beauty":
    the pivot at second, the pitch
      that can catch
the breath like Keats, Klimt, or Stravinsky.

Yet I'd seen only hard-edge lines,
    a cool green right-angle world.
      A child,
I ran from fiery disciplines,

playing ball with a boy's passion;
    but seeing her on the field
      with her child
as mother, catcher, second baseman,

feeling a pang as she held hands
    with her husband, I saw
      felicity
in Passions of the Renaissance

as well as in a double play,
    in the curves of Samothrace
      or Koufax
or her exquisitely made thigh.

Three years in dark hush I hid:
    my heart thumped — she lectured —
      our transport
when she'd say, "God, that's a gorgeous slide."

Ode to Apple Pie

I missed the figs last year.
By the time baseball was over,
the bush had lost its load of fruit,
leaving the ground sticky sweet
like bleachers after a game.

My teenager worked as a batboy
premier season of the local double-A team.
After three games, I knew their
names, numbers, positions.
After ten, their hometowns and vital stats.
Soon two were sent up to triple-A,
the knuckleballer on to the Big Show.
The deck of cards played in my head,
the catcher's Latin smile in my heart
or wherever is the seat of love at first sight.

Batboys learned the secrets.
The pair who set off firecrackers
behind the scoreboard.
The pitcher who stashed pine tar up his nose.
The third baseman scoring more
off the field than on.
Batboys were given tokens.
The usual balls and bats, caps and gloves,
cleated shoes and plugs of Redman chew.
After the final game,
Armando gave my son his catching gear, bag and all.
Just for fun, he slipped me his musky cup
to go with the signed tiger-print briefs
drenched in Eternity.

For eternity,
fresh muscles will stretch the jerseys, the stirrups.
The boys of summer will always average age 22.
This year
the catcher's outfit knights the corner
of my son's vacant room.
And under warm lids,
figs plump in amber juice.

A Softball Game

She is up at bat, he is in left field.
She is his teacher, he can
never have her. Every night
he dreams he has her,
every night he comes
in her arms, her skin
smells like passionflower,
her mind is hibiscus in summer
always flowering shockingly
beautiful. He goes
to her to ask advice about
his poems she bends over
them he looks at her
as if she were naked he learns
about ambiguity from her thighs,
how knowing when to break
a line is like knowing when
to enter when to withdraw
he learns about voice and song
from her sighs that enter
him like earth, and if only
she would come he would understand
epiphany.

But she will never
let him touch her she
smiles uncrosses her legs
gives him back the poem
marked with her
breath.

She has good arms she
slams the ball hard,
yes, it's how he would
do it to her the ball sings
like a good poem
it comes straight to
him he pulls his glove off
lets the ball slam itself
into his open
hand.

Listening to a Baseball Game
for Charles Baxter

The smothering heat of a July night
Squats in a second-floor bedroom
And doesn't move despite the desk fan's
Peaceful whir and simulate breeze.
A boy lies on the sheets and reads
A *Life* magazine which holds
The proper shadow of attention
While he listens to the ballgame
Being played in Kansas City.
He sees it happen and imagines it—
The same thing really. A car swings

Down Maple Street, a hinge complains.
Moths move toward decipherable light
But are stopped by screens. The boy's done
Reading and lies there beside the lamp,
His hands folded beneath his head.
He knows that comfort is rarely pure.
He listens and lets his feelings glide
With each intent description.
He follows a probable dream
As the night sways with outcomes
In houses and rooms and far away.

Singles

I don't know anyone more lonely
than the woman listening
to the late news, memorizing
baseball scores for coffee break.

She must undress so carefully,
folding her beige blouse
as if for the last time,
not wanting to be found unkempt

by detectives in the morning.
Sometimes I hear her talking
as she roams from room to room
watering her plumeria,

the only splash of color.
She sets two places at the table
though no one ever comes,
then turns to the boredom of bed

thinking *Indians* 7–*Yankees* 3,
Cardinals 11–Mets 2
until she rises before dawn
and drives crosstown to work.

Could anyone be more lonely?
She doesn't acknowledge, again,
the man in the tollbooth
who's spent the whole night there,

not even a magazine before him,
grateful now to be making change
and touching fingers, briefly,
with such a beautiful stranger.

Players

The beach made up
of sharp stones
reminds me
of a field
where I learned
baseball.
A bad hop
was always apt
to surprise
but not like this
topless beauty
kneeling to tend
her daughter's braid.
The child's blonde hair
fails to camouflage
the wedding band
that is as imposing
as a World Series ring.
I'm a young sailor
on liberty in France.
I'm used to sandy New England
shores and beach breasts
that are mysteries.
Standing, she leans
over to inspect her work.
Legs apart,
hands resting on knees,
she's a base runner
who just edged off first.
I gather lucky stones
and, skipping them off
the Mediterranean Sea,

I am a pitcher
checking her lead
when our eyes meet.

RINA FERRARELLI

Crowd at the Stadium

bits of flesh color   patches
of bright cloth   stitched
together in rows   in the old
fan pattern: a quilt
that rises in waves
with every cheering wind

In the Red Seats

High in the red seats'
vertiginous steep,
narrow rows, I stood
to let four drunks edge by,
and one, back turned to the field,
side-shuffled down the row,
shouting, "Hi! Great game!"
into averted faces.
Great game? It was nothing–
nothing in the first inning.
He breathed beer in my face. Our eyes
met and the force of meeting
seemed to tip him backward. He teetered,
flailed. I reached out, grabbed
his shoulder, pulled him erect
and past erect till we
were leaning forehead to forehead,
touching, and his eyes
flooded with love. He tossed
both arms around me, sobbed,
"You saved my life, man.
I swear I'll never forget you."
"Yeah, sure you will," I said
and slapped his back,
a quick, bluff way of saying,
"You're okay, pal" and "Hey,
let go." He nodded, shuffled
to his seat with his drunk buddies,
and one, as he slid past,
bobbed his eyebrows at me
and shrugged.

                    Five seats away,
from an adoring, pink,
intoxicated face,
love shimmered, love radiated
like equatorial sunshine,
the way a lover's face
illuminates the lover,
the loved, and the dark world
in one strange, lucent moment:
satisfied and thrilled, intense
and effortless — as God
regards us every moment.
I couldn't bear it. I left
in the fifth inning, sidling
down packed precipitous
red rows, easing past strangers,
excusing myself.

Supernatural

Heat and haze. The granular frayed-ends of late light
— the half-light of late afternoon, nearly evening —
and the dead center of a summer field. Heat-waves and dust.
Dust-haze. So the filthy leaves burnish like broken-in leather,
oily from a distance, and deepen when a breeze hits.

The percussive wood-crack—boys and girls run in the heat-waves,
wading, in a drift, as if underwater, through nothing
but more humid air. From where I stand petrified but happy,
holding a bat and starting to take my cuts,
this play of light has much to do with the way the scene

occurs: a figure on first, a figure, now held at second —
too few of us to fill the necessary field. And *ghost
runner on third!* a voice cracks, calling at my back
when I turn squinting outward into the cream sky.
This could be either memory or metaphor, you understand —

we are as close to love as we've ever been. Field-chatter.
A batter's breeze. All I have to imagine —
across the diamond's thistle and late steam, and dust-motes
like delicate sand afloat, and a distraction of nerves —
is what's already here, filling in for an absence

and particularized at will. A training ground for romantics.
So the boy with the bruised face knocks a bubble
of sweat off his lip, glaring at me, and begins his wind-up.
Desire can be this clarifying—down twenty-five years
and some fifty feet of heat-shimmer and loneliness,

light now like a lotion, a hazy presence at third becomes
a real runner, because we've wished it so—a run, if I'm lucky
enough to hit the pitch wobbling at me like a feather.
But there is one thing more. I'm looking down the line
as I swing—as far back now as my life goes—where the base still

blurs in the gray-white whirl. A ghost. A dazzle of white.
— Or the white-noise of what I've always wanted.—
Until it's you, of course, in the utterly breathless heat.
You, dug-in and grinning, as I swing—at this moment
when the field dissolves into tiny, abstract zeroes

and a backwash of vaporous light.
                                        Just like it's always been.
Heat and haze. You. Waving. Beginning to run this way.

MARK J. MITCHELL

Minor League Rainout, Iowa

Even today—the sun gone missing,

sky solid, sodden, all over gray,
wind bursting umbrellas—today

I can remember everything:
the small ball park in Iowa,
young athletes in cheap caps waiting
for the wind to stop, rains to go away

so a game could start. The grounds crew
smoking by the tarp spool (a drain
pipe, really), calm, ready to do
their act. And brats on coals, hissing
as raindrops pop their casings. Blue-
white lightning in the south, playing
tag with the light towers. The huge
river swelling, rolling away.

Even today—must be the storm—
while we walked the wet streets we knew
the game was holy and the rain
was sacred. We turned chairs facing
the Travel Lodge window, got warm,
watched the rain, the river, the blue-
black streets. Strangers from out of state
transfixed by weather, just sitting,
looking as clouds and lightning formed
new toys for God. I looked at you,
though you didn't know: wet, wild, fey
as you looked at the sky, wishing

there were words for this. Now transformed
into memory, it comes back, new,
borne by a cold and rainy day.
Your eyes, your wet hair, our kissing.

JIM DANIELS

Polish-American Night, Tiger Stadium
for H. G.

We sit with our girlfriends
in general admission, feeling like old guys
taking our wives to the ballgame — drinking beer,
eating kielbasa, talking about the future.
Twenty years old that summer — me, Debbie, you, Linda,
the summer John Hiller hurt his knee in relief
after striking out five in a row,
the summer you found out Linda liked the Carpenters
not the Kinks and wanted to become a CPA, so
you couldn't possibly get married
because you were obsessed with James Joyce and Ann Arbor,
the summer Debbie came on to you one drunken night,
then denied it later only to end up marrying Mike Dumbowski,
who despite being Polish was not there on Polish-American Night
and despite being my good friend
did not resist the advances of hot little Debbie,
who is now the secretary of her bowling league.

No, we did not know all this, just as John Hiller
did not know he would have a heart attack, but recover
to pitch well enough to become the Tigers' first star reliever,
even though tonight he'll injure his knee
and be out for the year.

The crowd was subdued after that.
The kielbasa was greasy and the wind was cold.
Debbie and Linda wanted to leave early,
so we did, without putting up a fight.
And it had started out so good, feeling a little like
old guys taking our wives to the game.

There's a risk every time you pitch.
Years later, you look back and can't figure it out.
Like what happened to our friendship.
But I'm glad you wrote me after many years
to find we still have much in common,
that we both have wives now who don't like the Carpenters,
aren't CPAs, and can be counted on
not to come on to our friends. Who was to know
with all that money Karen Carpenter
would starve herself to death? Maybe that's what
we were just beginning to learn that night,
that it can all come on so suddenly
just by bending your leg the wrong way.

Biographical Note

In the first game
of a twi-night
double-header,
July 10, 1947,
recovering alcoholic
Donald P. Black
of the Cleveland Indians,
only moments before
I slid safely into
the world,
fired a final
belt-high heater
that rookie
Ferris Burrhead Fain
waved goodbye to
for a no-hit,
no-run game,
rode the shoulders
of his team
into the dugout,
and disappeared
into the brightest bars
in the city forever.

JOSEPH BATHANTI

Softball

The field, boxed by a cyclone
fence, perches on a milltown bluff.
In left are apartments, blackened
from eighty years of ore dust.
A man on the third floor,
standing over a hotplate,
watches the stands fill early.
He never misses an inning.
The whole neighborhood is out of work,
taking it on by getting old.

The game starts with both teams
shoulder to shoulder, walking the field
for rocks and glass. No grass
to keep down the dust, the city
rolls it with oil that wells up
around the plate on a hot day.

We play once-real athletes
who let go their bodies for love
and doubling out on the open hearth.
Now they're broke, can't run,
but still have good eyes
and can kill the ball.

We end up losing
because we're small and out of town.
Our pluck is outdated,
uniforms too nice. After nine
we know a lot about them.
A loss would make them mean.

They know the mills
will never start up again.
In a fight we'd be pushovers.

This is nothing like baseball
where the mound is further from home,
and bases longer. The ball is big
and friendly. No one strikes out.
The only distant thing is the past.

MARY KENNAN HERBERT

Night Baseball, 1947

Enos Slaughter in left field
Musial in right field
the pitcher
warming up to the sound
of my brother's heartbeat
my father's voice
it is a lost July night in St. Louis
and my dress flutters behind me
as we run to catch a streetcar
after the game

THREE

A Baseball Game

Baudelaire went
to a baseball game
and bought a hot dog
and lit up a pipe
of opium.
The New York Yankees
were playing
the Detroit Tigers.
In the fourth inning
an angel committed
suicide by jumping
off a low cloud.
The angel landed
on second base,
causing the
whole infield
to crack like
a huge mirror.
The game was
called on
account of
fear.

September Pears

They thud to the grass
like long singles
to right field. Hard
as baseballs,
rain soon soaks
their skins, softens
the cores. Wasps
and white-tipped butter-
flies alight then,
as sweet rot
bloats the fruit
to softball size.
Swollen, they burst
into foul decay.
Yet crickets go on
chirping their approval
of the mottled corpses
scattered amid
pinestraw — memento
mori as jolting
as the electronic
scoreboard after
a fierce grand slam.

The Gamer

The line-up on the field is just like life.
We wear the uniform they tell us to
And stare into the camera, holding
Down the impulse to make faces or touch
The cups that hold our cocks and balls in place.
Straight-faced, competitive, we look like stitches
On a brand new ball. The game begins,
And when it does we'd rather die than lose.

It's like that at the office the next day
Where some ambitious one is coming up
Or someone spent is struggling, going down.
Either way, you're always in the way.
That's why your heart is pounding in your throat
As you drive home. Too stupid to say no
To one more drink before the family,
You suit up for the emptiness you own.

RON MCFARLAND

Photo of a Minor League Baseball Team, ca. 1952

In this photo of a semi-pro baseball team
the poet's the one who
looks like a poet
trying to look like a coach.

His arms are folded and he looks tough
in the shade of his cap.
Actually you can tell he does not quite
know how to be tough.

The guy smiling in the middle, wearing the dark
blazer and necktie,
owns the team. You can tell he does not quite
know how to smile.

The ballplayers all look manly and hard,
grim as a long, bad season
and terribly young. You can tell they know
exactly how to look.

Where Baseball's the Only Game in Town

Nothing could be as boring as it sounds,
the plains. Here, Comanches roamed a thousand years.
No one was safe. Landing, look out. You'll see

why they rode hard. The two-prop commuter drags
a long, straight-in approach and taxies across flat asphalt
to the shack, a squat brown terminal of mud.

Follow natives strangely in a hurry, a surly crowd,
and find your bags, a yellow cab outside, a skyline
lonely as you've heard, too gaudy wide to be the sky—

more like a laser show in the Astrodome. Nothing
for miles but fields of maize no taller than the car.
The ball-capped driver smokes and flicks hot ashes

in the breeze. Ignore the back-seat sign, *No Smoking*.
You'll find me sweating on one of four ball fields in town.
Bring a glove and beware: it's scrub, and we always

need good fielders who can run. You might stick in
a bat, just to be safe. And cleats, don't forget
a good, sharp pair of cleats.

Baseball Cards

that first baseball card I saw myself
in a triage of rookies
atop the bodies
that made the hill
we played king of
I am the older one
the one on the right
game-face sincere
long red hair unkempt
a symbol of the '70s
somehow a sign of manhood
you don't see
how my knees shook on my debut
or my desperation to make it

the second one I look boyish with a gap-toothed smile
the smile of a guy who has it his way
expects it
I rode the wave's crest
of pennant and trophies
I sat relaxed with one thought
"I can do this"
you don't see
me stay up till two
reining in nerves
or post-game hands that shook involuntarily

glory years catch action shots
arm whips and body contortions
a human catapult
the backs of those cards
cite numbers

that tell stories of saves, wins, flags, records
handshakes, butt slaps, celebration mobs
you can't see
the cost of winning
lines on my forehead under the hat
trench line between my eyes
you don't see my wife, daughter and son
left behind

the last few cards
I do not smile
I grim-face the camera
tight lipped
no more forced poses to win fans
eyes squint
scanning distance
crow's-feet turn into eagle's claws
you don't see
the quiver in my heart
knowledge that it is over
just playing out the end

I look back
at who I thought I was
or used to be
now, trying to be funny
I tell folks
I used to be famous
I used to be good
they say
we thought you were bigger
I say
I was

Geronimo at Short

After his surrender, Geronimo played baseball on the reservation.

He seems to disappear into the land
between the infield and the sweep of the grass.
Even the giant old trooper at the plate
has to look three times to find him.
Age has cut down his range.
Once, no line drive could escape his lunge.
His hands were where rallies and soldiers went to die.
He would play wildly out of position,
just to show them.
Spinning and shouting across the diamond
to kill the sure hit.
Now he must place himself well,
hiding in the dust,
stalking the vicious grounder.
He has stopped trying for balls
he knows he can't get.
Just spits and curses his teammates.
Even with all the years that follow him
he never looks when he throws.
Never.
It is always on target, always where it needs to be.
He relies on other things — the crowd's rustling
or the weight of the runner's steps — to tell him
what to do next.

He is still dangerous at the plate.
When the mood is on him, he can outwait anyone.
With the count full, he will foul off eighteen pitches
then get the walk
just to make the pitcher look bad.
His hits are always hard,

startling infielders or screaming into gaps.
On base he disappears again,
languid and silent, stealing without effort.
But when rage or booze takes him,
he plays another game.
The anger makes him expect
the ball's obeisance. Every pitch
supposed to do as he tells it.
He swings at bad throws. If he connects,
the other team is trapped by disbelief,
but mostly he jabs and misses,
betrayed by both slider and curve.
Those few times he drinks, he is sullen and uninterested.
Even then they are still afraid of him
and he draws intentional walks.
Then he takes the bat with him to
first base, holds it like a rifle and
sights it on the outfielders.

Something about Certain Old Baseball Fields

He doesn't know why he suddenly turns off the freeway,
steps out of his long, shiny car, drops his
keys that bury themselves in the soft dirt of the lot.
He tugs at the tie that's always knotted
at his throat, strolls to the middle
of the empty field where the sunlight strikes the outfield
like pale yellow music, where
grass blades applaud subtly in the wind.

He remembers standing on fields like these as a boy
in a frayed little-league shirt, his cap sideways on his head.
He'd run for that high pop-up,
a precious leather jewel he always seemed to catch.
He thinks how easy it is to miss
a life, to stand empty-handed beneath
an avalanche of sales slips and receipts and empty envelopes.

Now all those years fall away from him
like handfuls of torn papers
dropping lazily, silently into a deep canyon.
His three-piece suit seems to melt off, pool at his feet,
and he's naked.

He kneels down, curls up, as if pulled
by a cord that ties him to the earth of center field.
He feels the slow pain, then a sudden brightness
fills his eyes:
he takes the first quick gasp of air as the world
gently slaps him.
At last he can open his lungs
wide and cry, a cry that might, from across the field,
sound almost like a cheer.

JOSEPH DUEMER

Night Baseball in the American West
for Richard Hugo

Nothing echoes against the line
of blue hills except the announcer's
voice, wirey through the p.a. system
as a coyote's drawn-out twang.
It isn't much, these
dangled words, announcements —
it's all, the only game in a town
where local teams don't win,
where *visitors* beat the living
daylights out of downtown
streets with those big tires
made for rolling over dunes
like ripples on the surface
of a puddle, ripples on the scarred
surface of the earth, naturally
mute, which speaks only in stories
told by primitives across
a fire's sharp tongues;
but there are no primitives
where everybody wants big trucks,
bright chrome freckled with mud,
instead of the milky inside
of a girlfriend's thigh. Cleats
print the dirt around homeplate
with a kind of braille no girl's
hands hurt enough to understand.
The girl is only something
to put up there in the cab.
Now even losers get to play
in sodium vapor light that makes
the whole field look like

a television show. Wives
of the older players sit out
in the parking lot nursing
cold beers, long cigarettes,
black eyes, infants
whose keen howls turn pink
souls green even as some radio
preacher croons sweet Jesus
softly through the dark interior
and the windows start to fog,
turning the right field lights
to quiet fireworks. Far away,
the announcer tells who's next to bat,
and we mistake this for a ritual
when it's nothing but a dance,
when all we know is the score.

LAURENCE GOLDSTEIN

Is Reality One or Many?

No one would put it that way
anymore, as young Socrates did
and then endured Parmenides'
pontifical demonstration;
the more modern query is this,
from my eight-year-old son:
"Can a second baseman also
play left field? And who decides?"
The manager decides, I say,
taking the easy question first.
"Why? Can't he decide himself?"
I translate into Platonese:
Is every portion of a manifold
indefinitely numerous, or a unit?
And why is One set over Many
in this Republic more people
aspire to than occupy?

It's true, some play only one base,
one field — if well, they endure,
perhaps appreciate into All-Stars;
if badly, they are retracted
into one of us, the spectators
who may indulge in pickup games
or night-league shadow play
mimicking the true forms of the Leagues
but who are as much unlike
as like, for (Parmenides explains)
sameness and unity are different ideas.
A father is also a son, for example,
but not ever the son he wants to be,
the ideal son of his favorite myth,

nor his own son, in whose life
he participates with new-fledged hope.

By this time the boy slugger has fled.
I'm engaging myself in dialogue,
remembering how Parmenides proved
the One is in process of becoming
older and younger than itself,
like the whole ongoing law
and golden chronicles of the Leagues,
their sequence of rookies and veterans.
Baseball is One and Many at once,
offering all aspects of duration:
the diamond's luster cannot fade.

Hence happiness for my son,
not sinister as I was, conditioned
by weight and dexterity to first base,
trapper-mitt my sign of difference,
perishing *qua* professional in
the leaden echelons of the Pony League,
but one who throws with rectitude
and swings an outfielder's bat.
Another century will measure his powers.
What though my chance of glory has passed,
I am still his fellow amateur,
neither identical nor different,
having as we do a family resemblance
no less than Dodger with Dodger,
Twin with Twin, Free Agent with
some legend from the Hall of Fame.

There, our Symposium is finished.
The twilight gives us time
for some catch, a few innings
of the Tigers on live TV,
a bedtime story about the immortal Babe.

TONY COSIER

Southpaw

A twinge he did not like, a merest shade
Of feeling, as easily second to first they played

One out away from this game, a thousand outs
He hoped from his last one. With dance, with shouts

They fired a circle around him and lobbed him the ball.
He paced and stooped and tried not to recall

What his shoulder had almost felt. He fastened a lace
Halfway between the rubber and first base,

Not even a line near, no man's land but his,
The hope, the fear, the silence none but his

And the twinge he did not like, the merest shade.

Then, because there was nothing else to do,
He went back for the signal, kicked up a toe and threw.

DAVID CITINO

Returning to the Field

So many lovely things happen
in a field. This diamond, for example,
shaped by Queen Anne's lace,
clumped clover purple as a bruise
high on a delicate thigh. Buzz
of damselfly, chicory's azure.
The breeze is Mother's hand
riffling your hair. Gooseflesh.
Bubbles of dandelion, milkweed.

Beyond Hankins Container,
Continental Can, Precision Castings —
beyond even the new motels
of beaten drummers, city sinners,
you stride through the fence
to the backstop into a history,
dusty twists of rust-wrought wire.
You take your stance, Colavito's,
bat pointing fatally at the mound.

Head down, you run the bases,
full-bore sandlotter again, children
shouting you on, *Take second!*
Home! Home! Stepping on the plate,
lugging the flat mitt to first,
you muse the life you'll choose,
at ease with women and your own body,
all cash and steely wit, darling
of the neighborhood forever.

And now desire becomes clear.
Quarter of a century on, sparrows

trill long-familiar songs.
As you lie on your back, the body
admits at last it was fashioned
to fit this earth. Not even
clouds deceive. The language
of the field was time all along,
but you couldn't tell it.

DAVID FEELA

The Big League

The game barely started but
rain began singing its own kind of anthem,
a million teeth glistening in the bleachers
as if the sky could swallow an entire afternoon.
Jimmy's in the locker room
trying to grow up, showering with his buddies
while his father leans against the press-box window
moaning again about this distance he has come.
His belt is buckled under his belly
as he pushes the window open so the room can catch
its second wind and the sound of the locker room
drifts in, not far off, where the boys' coach can be heard
explaining how disappointment is a broken bat,
a stolen base, a bad call by the umpire.
It's a sin, the way Jimmy's mother crosses her legs.
They shine like chalk around the batter's box,
perfect enough to bring the bat boy
to his knees, send the earth spinning in the opposite
direction. She'll never use them for anyone
but Jimmy. He's the boy she most wants
to please. What is left of our desire but to sit
before our TVs, touch that place
where a player fumbles with his fingers,
holding a space knocked out of his life,
waiting for some big moment to happen.
Nobody wants to console Jimmy's father, not even me,
and my boy's the best friend Jimmy ever had.
I wonder if Jimmy's mother knows
how much she could mean to me.
When she touches her shoulder, then scratches her knee,
I'm trying to figure out what she means.
We must be like two planets, flung

from the center of our solar system,
twisting away from the sun as it disappears
behind a backyard fence, and I'm wondering
when my boy will be getting on home.

Visiting My Boyhood Friend after His Stroke

On our ball team, he played short with sweet ease,
and looked good even when he booted one,
pounding his glove, looking down at the webbing;
whatever chances came my way, I learned
from him to make a grace out of awkwardness.
When we played, our parents said we had potential,
believed in that grace we didn't have
and waited for, even if it never completely came to us.
One of us drove his car into a tree.
Another friend, good on the bases, died from cancer.
What is there to love about such impossible young men
if not the innocence we tried so hard to lose?
I treasure those years when we lived by our resilience,
the boys on our team, all of us dreamers —
even the slow-minded child who carried our bats
and the boy who loved magic so much that he learned
to make the things he wanted disappear:
I treasure those friends who shared with me
the diminishing summers when we couldn't understand
that what our parents liked to speak of as potential
was simply our capacity for coming up short,
and doing it with what they might have called style,
like our idols who leapt for photographers
with the balls already in their gloves,
and seemed to make spectacular catches in the air.

Hits

When the right fielder faded back for the fly ball,
we held our breath
and saw him step,
at the most inopportune time,
into a hole no one could have seen
and saw the long and lovely arc of the ball descend
to bash his head.
The boy slumped over his glove.
Parents ran from the stands and jumped cyclone fences.

Near the end of the season
we learned of a practice one team had across town.
A thunderstorm broke it up near the end,
and some kid, some rookie
happy about really tagging one off the coach,
or some team star, or somebody who wanted to do more
than sit in the dugout next game, or somebody
who'd been taught to do his share, some boy
was carrying the aluminum bats
to the coach's car.
They said you could trace his circuitous path
in the wet grass
right up to the point of impact.
The boy was in a coma for weeks.
Word was
the lightning burned a hole from his head to his feet.

If only I could believe there is a God or a Satan,
I could make something of these incidents
in a poem.
Satan, for example, for comedy, for sport,
can rearrange some dirt

and pick off any child he chooses.
And God, to no one's surprise, can hit a curve.

What I believe feels more like prose.

I believe the teammates of the boy struck by lightning go home and eat burgers and watch sitcom reruns. What else can they do, after the fact?

I believe the boy who hit the fly ball must learn never to break his stride as he rounds the bases on his way to home plate — even though parents race past him toward right field. When he dug up the batter's box with his cleats, he signed on to do a job.

I believe a good coach rises from bed at night and walks into his son's room, and walks into his daughter's room, and gives them signs they never see that are of no help at all and then utters the word "safe" over them.

I believe you and I stand on the field without glove or bat or catcher's cup or helmet. Something will be coming at us, as the coaches say, with "good velocity."

DAVID C. WARD

Isn't it pretty to think so?

Fathers playing catch
with sons:
as American as wheatfields mown
into ball fields
around which
great cities are built and on which
a golden light still
congregates
undimmed.

This father
playing catch
with this son: a stinging rebuke
sizzles in over
and over again, stitches thrumming
redly, welting a child's palm
from palm through arm to blood-fogged brain.
Pitching with intent: "Come on!
Be a man!"

I want to learn
and not be told and then have that telling
gilded in a myth
which smothers our unease
over beaten fathers
beating sons.

Catch

for my father

Sometime after supper
during my annual summer visit,
one of us uncovers
our battered Rawlings baseball gloves,
"the finest in the field,"
at the bottom of the foyer closet,
and we head out to the backyard,
lobbing a torn Spalding back and forth,
squatting and spitting
and shaking our legs to unlimber,
windmilling the stiffness
out of our arms between tosses
like aging relievers who can't remember
the last time they were summoned
with the game on the line.

Despite years of beer and cigarettes,
at some point you always declare
there's nothing I can throw at you
that you won't be able to catch.
As dusk descends we rear back farther,
smiles fading from our faces,
and uncork heaters low and hard,
scuffed cowhide exploding into leather,
to see who'll be the first to flinch.

The old anger at how we've failed
again and again in the clutch
to be what the other wanted surfaces
unspoken like the love between us,
each of your pitches cutting

imaginary corners finer and finer
till I sense how frightened you are
of all you might be forced to feel
should you ever lose your control.

Surprised and baffled one more time
by the flutter of your knuckler,
I bobble the ball and drop it.
My glove hand still stinging
from all those fast balls,
I turn away and curse you,
curse this game of saying nothing
neither one of us can win,
wind up and fling the ball back,
the curve you wouldn't teach me
to throw breaking in the dirt,
bouncing past you into the dark.

MICHAEL MCFEE

Old Baseball Found under a Bush

On this ultimate spitball
    steeped for who knows how many unseasonable seasons
      under a parkside bush,

two tiny snails are tracing
    fingerings: fast ball, slider, split finger, curve,
      a methodical rehearsal

over horsehide so putrefied
    the regulation pressure-wound muscular core beneath
      is dissolving like newsprint.

This is something you want
    to drop, not throw: the old flirtation with gravity
      has gone sour, there's too much

dirt and sweaty scuff and smell,
    the once-delicate swell of the never-ending stitches
      hidden in the pitcher's grip

protrudes like bones through skin.
    This thing was meant for the heavy hands of the dead.
      So I bury it under some leaves

as the snails polish their trail,
    a couple of umpires searching for whatever it was
      that made this ball jump once.

Everything But Everything

When Elizabeth at last accepts Darcy
  you've expected it so long
it's a surprise.
    You know everything
    except everything,
        as you know the copper beech
        will stretch
out in the sky but can't surmise
    each

gnarl, limb, or leaf.
    When I stand
out in left
    and we're far ahead,
    and Gary's got command
        of his slider, I see the game's grid
        laid
    over the ground,

over the green variables
of our skills
and lynx-alertness of our souls,
    how our beginning
        spins
    out of this three-out, nine-inning
        circumference
            we march into and then must wander
            through, the way a character
        in a romance doesn't know he's in a romance
        but takes ogres and dragons
as they come, as Dante sinks through circles
    believing

his goal's
> Beatrice
>> while obedient to the thorned structure
>> of the cosmos;

so the frame of the world depends
> on the horizontal dive at third,
>> on Jack's leap in right, his glove just clear
of the fence
>> to pluck the ball from air,
>>> and on the torque of wrist
that sends
>>> it sailing, each a local
>>> miracle
> without which this goodly structured
>> frame would not exist.

We sail into the unknown, you and I —
> have we sailed too far?
>> To navigate a marriage through the minors
>> is like voyaging
into the old North Atlantic: *Here There Bee*
> *Monsters,*
>> and we must guess
>>> the world is round, must suppose
> we'll keep striking shores
>> where we can trade
>>> in gold
> and take on fresh water,
> and as far
as what befalls you and me,
we watch the coastline and assume we know
>> everything but everything.

EDWARD R. WARD

Limited Power

allgame Tonig t
7:3 pm
Arkan as v. Shrevepo t

FOUR

KYLE LEE WILLIAMS

True Story

> I
> left her standing
> on 42nd Street
> pointing at the huge
> SONY screen, she said
> He's dead! He's
> Dead! Did you just see
> that! up there! Mickey Mantle.
> He just died! I just saw that,
> just now. Right here. While I was
> standing here next to you.
>
> Just now? I said
> isn't that something
> The Mick
> an era

RON VAZZANO

Baseball Haiku

Nine men stand waiting
under storm clouds that gather.
Someone asks for time.

Dreams Should Not Dog Great Center Fielders

who come in from the pasture.
Dreams should be pets gone fat.

In nightmares Mantle is
cramped, broad-shouldered,
in a taxi, hungry
as Mutt, his father,
who pitched his free time
to get Mick a ticket
from the mines.
He's late for the game, always.
　　And DiMaggio at the airport,
despite his tall grace,
eyes darting like some terrier's
as he stands beside his luggage,
glances at his watch;
he is late, as if he's waited years
to board a flight
that takes him back
to Marilyn.

And Mantle's dreams
can't shake the guards.
The announcer says,
"Now batting . . . number 7,"
as Mantle finds a hole
in the fence
but can't squeeze through.
　　And DiMaggio
for twenty-one years
sends six red roses
three times a week

to her Hollywood crypt,
but they're a dog's
nervous patter.

The dreams of the greats should
be tame, trained
to open and close a gate,
with Mantle strolling
his heaven in center;
Monroe on her toes,
smiling, leaning into
The Clipper's arms,
returning the roses of her
red lips.

The Career of Lou Proctor

*A press-box telegraph operator added his name and stats
to one box score and was subsequently listed in six editions
of the* Baseball Encyclopedia.

In 1912, for St. Louis,
his name in the box score.

He batted once — drew a walk,
was left stranded — but at the end

of the season that base on balls
fixed itself in records

as the career of Lou Proctor.
This Bible tells us so.

Six editions in all
where he's near the one at-bat

of Earl Pruess, who stole
a base after his walk, who scored,

unlike Lou Proctor, a run.
Holding this sixth edition,

we're dreamy with lies, though
even here, there's nothing

about birth or death, home town;
whether he batted right or left.

St. Louis Browns, we read,
American League; in the next

revision he's gone. This text
is the one to love: we learn

the modesty of Lou Proctor,
the accomplishment of fiction.

Question and Answer

After

Ralph Branca threw that 0–1 high and tight
fastball   not   quite   highandtight
enough trying to set up the low and away
curve (Sal Maglie said to him 20 years
later
If you wanted him to swing at the curve why
didn't you just throw him the damn curve)
and blew the pennant according to everyone but his teammates
he asked himself

lying face down on the clubhouse steps wishing

that they'd swallow him up

WHY ME   WHY ME   WHY ME

and he kept asking himself until he met up with his fiancée and
her cousin the priest who answered his question saying Because
God knew your faith was strong enough to bear this
cross and Ralph bought it and
now he makes all kinds of money sitting next to the guy who
made him a chump in '51 signing his name on baseballs.

He's a happy sixty-seven.

After

Donnie Moore tried to sneak one too many two-strike
fastballs past a dead fastball hitter and blew
the pennant

according to everyone including his teammates according to Donnie
even though they had two more
innings   plus
two more games

to get the job done he asked

himself over and over and over and over

WHY ME   WHY ME   WHY ME

and he kept asking but never found an answer never found a
line to buy into never found a way to bear the crushing weight
of his self-pity crucifix
no convenient cousin clergy explanation and
drugs don't answer questions they hide answers

he said I have become another Ralph Branca but Ralph is a happy
sixty-seven and Donnie was only 36 when he silenced
the questions.

He should've just thrown him the damn curve.

World Series, 1968, Southeast Asia

On the other side of the world
it don't mean nothin' —
the slow tedium of the pitcher
holding the ball in both hands
rubbing it as if it were a talisman
that could save his life,
and if the charm didn't work,
to lose it, just another game lost
in the box scores, a minor loss
buried in history; and the batter
tries to stay alive, waiting for that one pitch,
knowing there's another one out there
that has his number on it.

Men lose their gods at a time like this —
embrace the unthinkable — that gods die,
that men can kill them —1, 2, 3 — just like that.
It's never the same.

I turn away from the monotone
of the TV in the Officers' Club,
order another scotch and soda,
await the quiet ambush of that sweet drink
mixing the dream of Asia, new gods
charged with destruction
destroying the old gods because why not?
And losing it all doesn't matter
as the game dies like the loss of a friend
one has no time to mourn and that so easy anyway
in a game where deaths are recorded like outs
and neither the dead nor the living keep score.

Nothing moves in the heat, the alcohol stupor,
the wait. Lying back in the hootch,
I watch geckoes cling to the ceiling,
the only friends I trust now as I study,
dispassionately, the gods carving themselves
into pieces, and one of them turns and says,
"Who's next? What about you?" and laughs.

On the playground the ball
wants to be hit, to make everyone move
in the summer stillness, sunlight
curving through space,
folding a fly ball into the deep
field of sky, then falling back, under it,
waiting, watching the beautiful arc,
the beautiful white of the ball
against the beautiful blue of a cloudless summer.

This is no dream for a soldier
in times like these, the routine fly,
the line drive hit hard but right at him
so he doesn't move a step as the ball
slams into his glove with the sound and feel
that everything makes sense.

On the long flight back,
fields show certainly through the clouds,
the bases white as always, outfields still green
but so far away they're not worth coming home to,
not worth what it takes to get back.

To know this before returning
is the game one has to play,
the hard-won price of admission,
the accords one can never live up to.
It could have been Gibson on the mound

who held the ball too long, could have been
Cash or Kaline who stepped out of the batter's box—
whatever, it doesn't matter, the game slowed
past all time that matters in this world.

PAUL R. HAENEL

Short History of a Baseball

1.
It was never valued as a Tiffany egg
might have been but for years when I stole packs
of Luckies from my dad's top drawer
I'd see it in there

greying in places   smeared   but the stitches
still tight and blood red   seams precise
and parting just a small bit the way the earth's
crust bears promise to a plate-tectonics geologist

When I was a teen I'd think of it once in a while
whenever I played ball myself
but by then I was buying my own cigarettes
lifting twenty-nine cents from my mother's purse

and knew enough to leave the ball
where it sat wrapped in monogrammed
hankies   besides
I knew it would be mine eventually

In my twenties I thought of it once
I was making love   drifting far away
when the name Al Lopez came to me
out of nowhere

What's wrong honey
my lover said and I looked out the window
at a slate-grey Lake Michigan and said
Now who in hell is Al Lopez

When I was married I told my wife
the ball was ancient   guessed it'd been
my grandfather's who'd had a couple
try-outs as a catcher with the Pirates

I didn't know much about the history
of baseball   Mays and Mantle
Clemente   Maz   Big Stu   Stargell
who in hell was Al Lopez to me

2.
Last year my father handed me the ball
and recently he gave me his watch
It's with difficulty that he remembers Ruth's
last three homers at Forbes in thirty-five

I didn't know what to do with the baseball
I took it home   put it between two
hemispheres of plastic on a wooden base
and placed it on a shelf

It turns out Lloyd Waner's name
is on that ball   and Walter Beck
Bob Elliott   Max Butcher   a dozen
others and their handwriting is so beautiful

It turns out Waner was just a coach and the ball
was something my father's sister gave him
before he left for the Army in 1943
the 1943 Pittsburgh Pirates

those lucky bastards who were privileged
enough to know my aunt   a real fan
who hung around the dugout and was
sweet on Bob Elliott

I can just see my Grandfather shaking
trapped gas down his pant leg
a little nervous about his only girl hanging
around those ball players

nervous like he was back in nineteen
squatting behind the plate with a toy mitt
the better pitchers must have been nearly able
to ignite

You get a ball for your brother today
or perhaps she just loved him so
much she couldn't resist
the perfect gift

Play by Play

for Ernie Harwell, Detroit Tigers broadcaster,
1960—present

My grandmother holds onto Ernie's words, a gospel
of speared line drives, shoestring catches.
Robbed of a base hit: she curses softly.
Going, going, gone: she watches it sail.
Even at the ballpark, she squeezes her transistor.

She sometimes cries after a tough loss.
Ernie calms her, talks about
tomorrow's game, the starting pitchers.
Instant runs, she says
in the middle of making tea,
wiping the table. Or *Pull up a Strohs*
and stay awhile.

A small crowd on Ernie Harwell Day
cold rainy September. She stayed home —
applauded her radio. Ernie Harwell.
When he says *a man from Paw Paw*
caught that one, she sees that man spill
his beer, lunge across an empty seat.

She sees him driving west toward Kalamazoo
sipping coffee to stay awake, his son
asleep on his lap. Sees him smile,
palm the ball, check the runners,
throw a curve.

* * *

My grandmother turns up the radio
against her deafness, shoves the earjack in
a little deeper, wiggles it. *Ernie,*
where are you? she laughs nervously.

Tonight September wind breezes
in the open windows, a late west-coast game
drifting through the air. In the kitchen
I see the red glow of a burner she's left on.
I flick it off and peek into her dark room.
She is mumbling to herself
against the tinny static.
Let him hear her little prayers.

MICHELLE JONES

My Father, on the Day He Died

My father, on the day he died
    watched baseball
Tigers at White Sox, WGN,
    as they wheeled him into ICU.

As he had his heart shocked
    and refused a respirator
I watched a game on ESPN.

My husband, not a gambling man,
    asked
        what are his chances?

I watched a succession of pitches
    stats
    replays
    commentaries
trying not to remember
trying not to forget

Tried not to picture his big hands
    pierced by IVs

(In labor I'd thought about Trammell
    twitching, shifting,
        settling
    to rap out a double.

Blue sky, green grass, fresh air.)

A college first baseman
    smart hitter

Later an umpire
  the good kind
  you don't notice.

My father had phoned me
  his hospital to mine.

The baby cried.

Sounds like he's got
  a good set of lungs,
  he said.

I wear a T-shirt of his
  as I write,
the baby squirms on my lap.

Baseball in Ohio

Reaching for the bat, he wasn't thinking
about the Series he'd listened to when he was nine,
afternoons flopped on the parlor floor,

the rasp of the announcer's voice
and the rush of leaves he'd neglected to rake
hurled against the screen door.

He couldn't even remember whose bat it once was,
exactly, and the initials burned into the heel
could have been any one of the boys' names

and the fingerprints might have been his own,
those divots and scuffs from the sandlot games
or someone's Little League championship

if they'd played Little League. It was all blurred now,
who wore a gray cap, winter and summer, and
which one he'd had to whip for telling his mother to shut up.

He found the bat in the basement, after managing
all those stairs, groping along dusty rows of peaches
that hadn't exploded with the others fifteen years back,

drawn to it, knotty fingers aching for the feel
once more of the solid wood, the weight and heft
of the bat, the wrists and arms remembering.

Too frail for many practice swings, and no room, really,
among those cartons and tools and Christmas decorations,
he mustered his strength on the stairs and connected

with the back of her head, poised against the recliner cushion,
caught the satisfying crack, the sting in the shoulder
and arms and the silence, the silence at last.

Betting on the Muse

Jimmy Foxx died an alcoholic
in a skidrow hotel
room.
Beau Jack ended up shining
shoes,
just where he
began.
there are dozens, hundreds
more, maybe
thousands more.
being an athlete grown old
is one of the cruelest of
fates,
to be replaced by others,
to no longer hear the
cheers and the
plaudits,
to no longer be
recognized,
just to be an old man
like other old
men.

to almost not believe it
yourself,
to check the scrapbook
with the yellowing
pages.
there you are,
smiling;
there you are,
victorious;

there you are,
young.

the crowd has other
heroes.
the crowd never
dies,
never grows
old
but the crowd often
forgets.

now the telephone
doesn't ring,
the young girls are
gone,
the party is
over.

this is why I chose
to be a
writer.
if you're worth just
half-a-damn
you can keep your
hustle going
until the last minute
of the last
day.
you can keep
getting better instead
of worse,
you can still keep
hitting them over the
wall.

through darkness, war,
good and bad
luck
you can keep it going,
hitting them out,
the flashing lightning
of the
word,
beating life at life,
and death too late to
truly win
against
you.

Telephone Call

When Emma heard him say he didn't love her,
she thought of spring,
she thought of a spring without baseball,
what it would be like if boys who lived in towns
with names like Idabel, Osceola, or Tonopah
held smooth round rocks in their hands
without knowing how such a small dream
can send a boy to a city
of lights and noise and grateful women,
or what it would be like if the girls
who loved them never knew the hard bleachers,
or the anxious taste of chewed pencils,
never kissed boys who left the dust
from a slide on their skin,
or what it would be like if fathers never knew
how old they were because their arms
didn't weaken, their shoulders, backs never slipped,
their sons earned pride or sadness or shame
in some less simple way,
or what it would be like if mothers
didn't stand at kitchen windows and see
their boys learn that women watch,
that a good woman will ride
all the way across the state
with a game on and never
ask for music.
When Emma heard him say he didn't love her,
she thought of dresses she had never worn.

ROBERT GIBB

Williams in Autumn

October 4, 1961
          The hawkweed is bristling
In the Jersey meadows
          And the sidewalks of East Rutherford
          Are littered, here
          And there, with hulls
From the horse chestnut trees.

The end of summer
          Is no poorer for any of that.
The cemetery's snow-faced doughboy
          Stands overlooking the pastures
          Of his republic,
          And at 9 Ridge Road
The old poet,

Beautiful and bare of poetry,
          Has finally declined to rummage
Through the welter of his years.
          He is tired of being a house
                    Whose rooms are closing,
          Stroke after stroke,
          And wants now simply to sit

Bathing in the light
          He thinks is falling
For the last time into Yankee Stadium,
          Flooding the shapes of the players,
                    And spilling into the room.
          A game he wrote was *close*
          to the principles of physics

and lyric poetry.
Four innings later
New York breaks on top,
One to nothing, Ford's unfurling body
Flashing homeward, again
And again, an abacus
Of pure, blurred beads.

And Williams elated
By the seeming spontaneity
Of such control,
The pattern to its variations,
As in jazz
Or local speech.
In the bottom of the sixth,

The Yankees double their lead.
The game flows slowly
Through the line-ups one last time,
As though it meant to go on forever,
The slant light falling,
It seems to him,
Like something from Masaccio,

The *Expulsion* perhaps,
The way it bathes the lit,
Attendant figures
Who are about to step out of Eden
Into the world of time —
NEW YORK 2–CINCINNATI 0 —
Of traffic and the evening news.

October Play

Even before the batter's hips twitch,
before the bat's whirled and the crack
jump-starts the crowd, he knows,
the only one in the stadium
whose back is to the ball arcing up and up and out.
He gives that unmistakable grudging look,
classic as the batter's swing,
up only so far as his forward stance allows
and then down into the hand that betrayed him.

All he wants is the unscarred ball
back in his mitt,
as we want to retrieve
our wild words, the inside hurt, truth
hurled so cleanly down the middle
it can't be missed.

Like the pitcher wintering his error,
we run out our lingering grudges,
shout to moving air, walk
over chittering leaves to stand
scuffing dirt
in front of worlds we imagine
entering. We wait there
for something to turn us around —
a familiar sign, a sound —
something in the knowing when it's safe
to let go and go home.

Night Baseball

*[I] retrace by moonlight the roads where I used to
play in the sun.*
— Marcel Proust

At night, when I go out to the field
to listen to the birds sleep, the stars
hover like old umpires over the diamond,
and I think back upon the convergences
of bats and balls, of cowhide and the whacked
thumping of cork into its oiled pockets,
and I realize again that our lives pass
like the phased signals of that old coach,
the moon, passing over the pitcher's mound,
like the slowed stride of an aging shortstop
as he lopes over the infield or the stilled echo
of crowds in a wintered stadium. I see again
how all the old heroes have passed on to their
ranches and dealerships, that each new season
ushers in its crop of the promised and promising,
the highly touted and the sudden phenoms of the
unexpected, as if the hailed dispensation of gifts
had realigned itself into a new constellation,
as if the old passages of decrepitude and promise
had been altered into a new seeming. I remember
how once, sliding into second during a steal,
I watched the sun rest like a diadem against the
head of some spectator, and thought to myself
in the neat preutterance of all true feeling,
how even our thieveries, well-done, are blessed
with a certain luminousness, how a man rising
from a pilfered sanctity might still upright himself
and return, like Odysseus, to some plenitude
of feast and fidelity. It is why, even then, I loved

baseball: the fierce legitimacy of the neatly stolen,
the calm and illicit recklessness of the coaches
with their wet palms and arcane tongues of mimicry
and motion. It is why, even now, I steal away
from my wife's warm arms to watch the moon sail
like a well-hit fly over the stadium, then hump
my back high over the pitcher's mound and throw
that old curve of memory toward the plate
where I run for a swing at it—the moon
and the stars approving my middle-aged bravado,
that boy still rising from his theft to find the light.

ED MARKOWSKI

My Last Hit

Late at night
I can still
see the ball

arcing

over the third
base bag, just
inside the line,

hugging

the grass. The
fielder frozen solid,
his mitt a

heavy

stone, resting on
his thick knee.
And that was

it.

Dream of a Hanging Curve

When I see it spinning
like a Florida grapefruit
toward me, let me not
lunge at it like a rookie.

If it's outside, help me
shift my weight and lash
it to the opposite field.

If it should come down
the middle, let me send it
right back where it came
from, but harder and faster.

If it comes toward the inside corner,
give me the patience to wait,
turn on it, and pull it down
the line to kick up chalk
and carom around in the corner.

If I should have the luck
to make the right connection,
follow through perfectly
and see the ball rise
in an arc that will end
somewhere behind the fence,
let me not take too long
to circle the bases, gesture
toward the other dugout,
jump onto home plate,
or high-five everyone in sight
while the pitcher hangs his head.

If this dream comes true,
do not let me expect it
will ever happen again.

Do not let me change
what I have been doing
that got me to where I am.

Let me stay here as long
as I can give what I have
been given to contribute.

Let me be remembered
for what I became,
not for what I might
or should have been.

America without Baseball

When baseball died,
back in the twenty-first century,
Americans were too maddened with grief
even to go to the funeral.
Instead, they raced backwards around the bases
again and again, subtracting a run,
each time a foot hit home plate,
from 1839, the year baseball was invented.
Reaching zero, they fell down and wept,
released from their long slump of denial.

With baseball gone, Americans could see
that the moon had become a towering
fly ball, possibly a home run,
though the line between fair and foul
had been obliterated for all eternity.

Soon, box scores began to look
like Greek or Sanskrit so that someone
chancing upon them in yellowed newspapers
could have been meeting an old flame,
the embers cold, and wondering
what he had possibly seen in her.

The word "fungo" disappeared
from the language except in the dreams
of a few Americans where it was uttered
by a stranger who came at them
angrily waving a club,
or else the word emanated from a rock
sea water had begun to shape into a perfect sphere.

3 and 9 became magical numbers —
all automobile license plates
carried either or both,
as did the logos of some commercial ventures,
though often buried in the design
to work subliminally on customers,
though no one could remember why.

The crack of the bat
traveled the universe
as an ambiguous signal picked up
from deepest space,
and the radio and television announcers'
measured drone as the ball speedily
toured the field in a series of sharp
angles, hand to wood to wall to
hand to glove, sank
to be a hum at the earth's core,
a basso continuo from which seismic activity
got an assist.

Some prophets appeared
speaking of the second coming
of America's favorite pastime,
but passersby left them
stranded on street corners
like base runners on second and third,
the side retired.

Only the flowers showed up
for spring training,
impressing everyone with their knowledge
of the fundamentals, and in mid-summer
the batting averages
of the corn, the stars, and the rivers soared.

In fall, when the World Series once
filled the calendar,
lovers abed
passed the hours
with the best of seven caresses.
And as winter approached, Americans everywhere
listened to their heartbeats
scoring over and over
and felt for the first time
released into free agency.

GEORGE LOONEY

Tired of Loss and Sin

Last night you flew over water no sin could
turn ugly with rumors of old men in love
with nothing but the wreckage of a team
they can't stomach, coughing over pale beers.
Tonight, the news says nothing about planes
falling from the sky. The local team lost
again. You slept through it, Lake Superior
a confession in a dream where your penance
was to name your son for the awkward center
fielder of the local team the year you rode

a rusted bike down a dirt path and spent
hours in the woods in what was almost
passion, crushing grass into patterns you liked
to say were hieroglyphs some god read at night
to believe in himself. Now and then
he brought a radio rolled up in the blanket,
and you'd listen to the local team lose
while he touched you. There are teams everywhere.
Even the northern states. Where you've gone,
they're on a streak, sixteen and counting. Your sister

knows all the players' names. She's in love with
the center fielder, and chants his stats
with beers on her balcony, telling you
about a double play last night. *Like a prayer,*
she says. *Like absolution.* While you flew over
a body of water large enough to hold
your guilt, two men formed a single definition
of grace, and your sister's center fielder
waited for anything to come down to him
out of a sky that was never enough

to hold anyone. Your sister says it's almost
a sin, how the team can do no wrong, the beer
getting to you. You say swallows are
flying from eaves into the dark. She laughs,
says you're drunk. Here, old men whose team
can't win stumble home. Beer on their breath
angers women tired of the talk and the slow
despair of losing. Your sister tells you love
has a mean slider, and a curve that breaks
at the last second. Our bodies say the laws

of physics can't be broken, and we fall out
of the box in front of a perfect pitch. So much
is illusion. Your sister's drunk and asleep.
Old men mumble, drunk. It seems the world is
breaking them, every fly ball lost in the sun,
and they can't beat out a bunt no matter how
well they lay it down. The players dream of
women who whisper in foreign tongues, loss
not a word they know, their exotic mouths
perfect wells to wish down. The players want to

confess they never cared about winning. *Rumors,*
your sister says asleep, *can kill a streak.*
A swallow's chest glows in stray light. Rumors,
you've learned, can kill most anything. Old men
slip naked under blankets and dream wives
turn to them without anger. Your sister
sleeps, breathing the name of her center fielder
as though his grace could absolve her. Confession,
you've decided, is a curve ball that doesn't
break. And sin doesn't play but goes to the games

and heads home after downing a last warm beer.
Flying home, you could transcribe hieroglyphs
light draws on the water and believe
you've confessed every sin, water a rumor

of absolution. But tonight, the local
team's winning. The news says it's the bottom
of the ninth, the visitors down to their last out.
I imagine a fly ball to deep center. Maybe
sin isn't what any of us think it is. The love
your sister has for the center fielder with no errors

is something you'd like to feel. To be that sure
of anything. Here, the center fielder takes
the fly ball to retire the side and end the game,
the first win in weeks. And old men
are absolved by women stroking the white hair
of their sunken chests while, under the water
you crossed, centuries of loss rust in ships
men bet their lives on. Maybe this is a confession.
Maybe Confession's where I have to go,
the neighborhood bar named by a monk who left

the monastery for a woman he said was
an angel. When she died, the sky was the color
of sin. Rain for weeks without end. They had
to wait to bury her, the ground too soaked
to stand up to digging. The monk believes in
the team, his regulars old men who cough
like she had at the end. Even angels get tired
of loss. And sin, the monk says to the last drunk
left, is the dark in pictures they took when she was
getting worse. We bet our lives against loss,

and we lose. Confessing doesn't absolve us
of anything. The sky that held you last night
was a prayer an ex-monk's whispered every night
for years before sleep. Angels do come down
to us, and no sin can deny their grace.
Tonight, old men dream they lie with angels.
In the morning they'll believe their love
was the difference, not the simple grace of

the center fielder's glove. Tomorrow I'll close
Confession with the ex-monk and believe

the only sin is the distance between us.
The local team will win again. Old men will go
home early and hold angels for luck. There'll be
love and rumors of love as long as the team
wins. It will seem we've been absolved of sin.
Blessed, the ex-monk will say, believing
in such things. I won't argue with him,
or tell him I believe touching you is
the only forgiveness. This isn't a confession,
but a prayer. That the sky holds you safely home.

DONNA J. GELAGOTIS LEE

Winter at the Ball Field

The ball field
stretches out into
the park, its baselines
long legs.
In the armchair of winter
it relaxes, the tracks
of birds and small
animals tripping up
the baseline. The sun
opens itself
fully overhead
like the home run
of summer. I am sitting
on the bleachers. I have
dusted off a seat. The
wind cheers for me
as I watch the memory
of summer white out.

FIVE

World Series, Game 5

Even God, I think, is here,
so high up in the stands
with my ten-year-old daughter and me
we can almost touch the X
from Schmidty's old home run,
probably the two worst seats at the Vet
but right where the whole world
wants to be.
I let her drink real Coke,
eat Milky Ways and dance with strangers
at 11:30 on a school night and still
ninety minutes from home.
I hold her sticky hand.
The Phillies and we are in control.
For now, the world has stopped worrying
about players who might be traded,
moods that might swing and miss.
There are no thoughts about new uniforms
and the boys who will wear them.
Tonight she is here and finds it easy
to love me for this end-of-season
home game.
We are those jumping red dots
in the center of the universe, my daughter
and me and a baseball game
that is perfect and no more meaningless
than anything else.

KAREN KEVORKIAN

Softball Dreams

I did not know why I liked it, all the waiting,
then the ball falling from the sky
smacking my glove, forcing from it
a scent like a shoe's inside,
the glove's new lacing creaking
like ship rigging.

I studied the sky above
the bill of my red cap,
the jets detailed as toys
that crossed silently
but seemed near collision,
the shrieking birds that were a river
of black beating shapes. One night
the sky and the dirt were the same color.
I moved with the ease of a swimmer
through the cool ruddy element,
the ball always a surprise
rushing into my face.

All women, we began playing in the evening
in those long hours after dinner.
Considering each other
only according to skill, we played
until the sun, orange and solid,
was eclipsed by trees. At the edge
of the diamond our children spraddled,
through fists trickling sand,
filling bottles.

On the hot nights I would wake
uncertain in my own bed
as if standing on a midnight riverbank,
water sensed
by its sheen through trees.

The schoolyard was enclosed
by maroon brick houses, their small porches
overflowing with red and purple petunias.
Each pavement crack was tufted
with spider-rampant grass.
A dense season, the air thick
with moisture and kicked-up dust,
overripe figs in the alleys dangling
under the coarse, splayed leaves.

When we could no longer close our dry mouths
we'd go to a bar where a mirrored ball
revolved in green light, its phosphorescence
shattering on our faces, and beneath
the feet of the dancers
who pulled near each other,
without intensity, underwater.

Voices of the Sea

The sea has many voices,
Many gods and many voices.
— *T. S. Eliot, "The Dry Salvages"*

The barker filling the boardwalk arcade
with promises played first base when I played
third. His hands were soft as a god's when he
dug low throws from the dirt. I heard he stayed
home, turning down an offer from Boston
so he could help his aging father run
the family fish market.
                              He tells me
knocking down metal bottles will be fun.
He thinks I can win my choice off his shelf
for the little boy there, or for myself
from underneath the counter.
                              Then I see
that he sees me. As the speedster from twelfth
grade hovers in salt air between the child
and man before him, his laugh becomes wild
as a gull's above the rock jetty.
This was the solemn boy who never smiled?

He makes me remember autumn's hoarse voice
at high tide heard from my porch, spring's voice
of sudden squalls and sighs as winter seas
surged against the low dunes. But summer's voice
still eludes me.
                              I have come home to hear
it once more, bringing my son and an ear
trained to other sounds. I wanted to be
beyond memory, to float without fear
again in the Atlantic at midnight

thinking of nothing more than the lone light
at land's end.
         I thought it would be easy,
coming back with my son, at last the right
frame of mind — everything in place to hear
what the sea was saying and make clear
the lost sounds that had long been haunting me.

MICHAEL S. HARPER

Archives

Cooperstown, N.Y.

Photos and clippings fade;
no one can find a real signature
of Rube Foster, who put together
the Negro Leagues; efforts
at why Josh Gibson died at thirty-
five are even vaguer,
his sleek strong body in the waves
of San Juan the vintage year:
1934. Later, 72 home runs,
the only ball over the third tier
at Yankee Stadium
for the games on off-days.

No flicks of Gibson as a Globe-
trotter, his golden gloves
astride the mound captured,
for real, with Curt Flood,
eating steaks on a grill,
in a parking lot in spring
training. Reggie is a mask,
astride a roadster, a paltry
lid on a rainday with Vida Blue.

Frank Robinson's loaded automatic
put him under arrest; the flick
of his headrag, a white mop,
only shown in Cincinnati,
eating Satchel's 45-lb. catfish,
chasing "Willmont" Liquors, Inc.
as endorsements in Brooklyn.

The clippings of the rest
of Negro America are full of glee;
no ounce of bitterness,
except for Jackie, who hit
better than they thought,
and was fast, stealing home
in public, voting Republican,
the whole Civil War
on his back and pigeon-toes.

On PBS the documentaries,
one trailer sideshow,
a whole hall of oral history
in transcriptions
of black and white.

Trujillo, who paid the best,
threatened execution if you lost;
the black World Series in Comiskey
full of chicken, zoot suits,
trainfare from everywhere
but endorsements, turnstyles.

"Let's play two."

Poem for My Father
for Quincy T. Trouppe, Sr.

father, it was an honor to be there, in the dugout with you
the glory of great black men swinging their lives as bats
at tiny white balls burning in at unbelievable speeds
riding up & in & out
a curve breaking down wicked, like a ball falling off a high table
moving away, snaking down, screwing its stitched magic
into chitling circuit air, its comma seams spinning
toward breakdown, dipping, like a hipster
bebopping a knee-dip stride in the charlie parker forties
wrist curling, like a swan's neck
behind a slick black back
cupping an invisible ball of dreams

& you there, father, regal as african obeah man
sculpted out of wood, from a sacred tree of no name no lace origin
thick roots branching down into cherokee & someplace else lost
way back in africa, the sap running dry crossing
from north carolina into georgia, inside grandmother mary's womb
who was your mother & had you there in the violence of that red soil
ink blotter news gone now into blood & bone graves
of american blues, sponging rococo
truth long gone as dinosaurs
the agent-oranged landscape of former names
absent of african polysyllables, dry husk consonants there now
in their place, names flat as polluted rivers
& that guitar string smile always snaking across
some virulent american redneck's face
scorching, like atomic heat, mushrooming over nagasaki
& hiroshima, the fever-blistered shadows of it all
inked, as body etchings, into sizzled concrete
but you there, father, through it all, a yardbird solo

riffing on bat & ball glory, breaking down all fabricated myths
of white major-league legends, of who was better than who
beating them at their own crap game with killer bats
as bud powell swung his silence into beauty
of a josh gibson home run skittering across piano keys of bleachers
shattering all manufactured legends up there in lights, struck out
white knights on the risky slippery edge of amazement
awe, the miraculous truth slipping through
steeped & disguised in the blues, confluencing
like the point at the cross
when a fastball hides itself up in a shimmying slider
curve breaking down & away in a wicked sly grin
curved & broken-down like the back of an ass-scratching uncle tom
who like old satchel paige delivering his famed hesitation pitch
before coming back with a high hard fast one, rising
is sometimes slicker, slipping & sliding
& quicker than a professional hitman—
the deadliness of it all, the sudden strike
like that of the brown bomber's short crossing right
or the hook of sugar ray robinson's lightning cobra bite

& you there father through it all, catching rhythms of chono
pozo balls, drumming like conga beats into your catcher's mitt
hard & fast as cool papa bell jumping into bed
before the lights went out

of the old negro baseball league, a promise you were
father, a harbinger, of shock waves, soon come

If You Know Me at All

I once prayed that this acre be the elm's home,
but my elms are dying, or dead. Today I dragged
almost the last torso to the back line
for mouse- and rabbit-shelter over the long winter.

Babe Ruth, whose decorum on formal occasions I sometimes
for the health of my soul have needed to emulate,
said near his end that termites had gotten into him,
and as I hauled elm bats away across autumn,

my right elbow and left knee ground out their lamentation.
But I am used to them by now, and almost
unafraid. Me and the Babe and the elms got
a season or so to go before we're nothing here

but sawdust. I root for them, as you will,
with me, if you know me at all. In elm bark we see
children on diamonds over which the sun passes,
and all our home runs in the cross-cut growth rings.

DONNA J. GELAGOTIS LEE

Final Play

the pitcher winding up—
the sun throwing
his shadow

Why I Love Baseball

Working my hand into one of those stiff
four-fingered gloves designed for
second basemen, I wonder why
even before the strike, so many people
turned against baseball,
favoring the quick kill,
raw meat, cracked bones, and twisted ligaments
of football.

We have become impatient.
We have lost our enthusiasm
for the subtle, the elusive,
the comfort of peanuts and
sunflower seeds and the sweet
boredom of a summer afternoon.

When I was about eight
my brother had a glove like this, a glove
that seemed to harden
in the sun.
Nothing could break it in, and when one
golden afternoon he left it stranded on second,
it never returned,
but he came back a few years down the road
unscathed from Vietnam with a story of how he was
left on second with two out and the score tied
when the mortars fell on Pleiku.

Another brother I know of
apparently tried to field a Cong grenade,
maybe a basket catch like Willie Mays.
But I don't know how much he loved the game.

Gloves like this one hold the hand steady,
as if Rogers Hornsby himself were
holding your hand firmly to the dirt
for a hot grounder years before the war.
With an old glove like this and a new baseball,
you could start the whole world over.

LINDA GREGERSON

Line Drive Caught by the Grace of God

Half of America doubtless has the whole
of the infield's peculiar heroics by heart,
this one's way with a fractured forearm,
that one with women and off-season brawls,

the ones who are down to business while their owner
goes to the press. You know them already, the quaint
tight pants, the heft
and repose and adroitness of men

who are kept for a while while they age
with the game. It's time
that parses the other fields too,
one time you squander, next time you hoard,

while around the diamond summer runs
its mortal stall, the torso that thickens,
the face that dismantles its uniform.
And sometimes pure felicity, the length

of a player suspended above the dirt
for a wholly deliberate, perfect catch
for nothing, for New York,
for a million-dollar contract which is nothing now,

for free, for the body
as it plays its deft decline and countless humbling,
deadly jokes, so the body
may once have flattered our purposes.

A man like you or me but for this moment's
delay and the grace of God. My neighbor
goes hungry when the Yankees lose,
his wife's too unhappy to cook,

but supper's a small enough price to pay,
he'd tell you himself, for odds
that make the weeks go by so personal,
so hand in glove.

Listening to the Ballgame

Here, in what one poet called
     The realm of decline, among
Momentary days, I stretch out
     On the couch, close my eyes,
And listen as the game gathers
     Its dimensions of clarity
And grace. An east wind
     Billows through the curtains.
The light of Saturday afternoon
     Spills into the room, shining
On the round leaves of the ivy.
     What is time to me? The surf
Of voices drifts against my ear
     And is sea enough, and memory.
Just this morning a red bird
     Fluttered against my window
Like a battered heart trying
     To get back home. Now my wife
Sings in the kitchen, slicing
     Red berries into a bowl.
The child she carries is red
     And translucent with blood
As the sun inside my eyelids,
     And the day arcs above us all:
Cloudless, cornflower blue.

A high sky, the players call it,
     Where spheres fall from light.
So much of what we love takes
     Place beyond us, I'm grateful
For each of these returning
     Curves, for the calculus

By which Clemente drifts back
   Toward the right-field wall
And the ivy flashes like flakes
   Of bronze in old Forbes Field.
I don't know what that bird
   Meant to tell me, or whether
I'll ever stop comparing
   The loss of a ball park to
The fall of Troy. Or how long
   My momentary days will continue
To fill with such splendid ease.
   I think about the nine round
Stations we pass through, out
   Of that only paradise, into
The realm of decline. Of how
   There are moments in which
The world, which never promised
   A thing, returns instead
Enough to curve us into song.

The Cure

baseball is a good antidote for death
where else do we mutter belief scream
hope over green grass bathed
in light where else do we coach the best
out of one another

it's all right baby
you can do it
settle down guy
you'll be okay just hang in there
we need you buddy
we need a spark
be the ignitor man

our whispered pleas combine over rows
of seats and peanut calls and pour into the ears
of our boys fixing them
with our best hope the best we have to give

nowhere else do we do this together
reverently from some untapped place
in our chests saved for our children
and our lovers we thought we'd used it up
but listen to us croon making our voices
carry just the right mixture
of love and demand

our throats are sore
the peanut shells under our feet flattened
from jumping up and sinking down again
our hearts extended

pumping belief
into this one afternoon

you can do it
you can do it for us
do it now come on
do it now

JOEL LEWIS

A Dharma Talk by Johnny Roseboro, Boulder, Colorado, March 23, 1983

The permanent hairline
that Juan Marichal
grooved into my scalp
with the trademark side
of his Louisville Slugger
is not the scar I show
for the dozen years
of my scuttling ways
along Backstop America.

I was not meant
for the Hall of Fame
but, still, one of the best
of my era. I began as shade
for the great Roy Campanella
& later, under the crackling
Chavez Ravine sun, caught
the greatest pitching staff
of its time: Koufax, Drysdale,
Podres, with Ron Perranoski
in occasional relief. I remember
Koufax's impossible sidearm curve,
and the packed stands
of common folk
& Hollywood celebrities
cheering our best moves.

& I still remember
those late days of radiance
playing out my career

as bench jockey
for the lousy Senators,
cooling in the dugout
toying with my three
World Series rings perched
like clementines
on my fingers.

But here at the Zendo
I realize that all my
Golden Gloves, hero plaques & winter rubber chickens
were physical graffiti
in a world of samsara.

What really mattered was the plain
joy of fielding a pop-up by the dusty
lip of the dugout and employing
zen mind to draw a walk.
And how beautiful
were the grey chrysanthemums
that base runners create
as they slide into home plate,
their spikes up, my fat mitt low,
that not-thinking of doing
when the samurai
comes out of us all.

And although I can't claim
constant radical compassion,
my heart is tuned to the rhythms
of these mountain neighbors
of Boulder Creek past the door
of new green rising on Baseline Road
of gloved hands across America
plucking white Haitian apples
out of March's moody air.

Carolina League Old Timers Game
for Miles Wolff

Their dead arms cock and toss
ghostly looping baseballs.
With golf-course tans,
observable paunches,
and bored teenaged children
in the stands,
they trade anecdotes
their wives will never hear.

In the dugouts,
young minor leaguers
giggle, not recognizing
how it is they will gather
their own aged summers
into a blue-weather
three-inning old timers game
where the trails cross
past pink slips, real jobs.

In our dugout,
Joe Cowley farts
and says Enos Slaughter
is obscenely fat.
Out on the mound,
Tommy Byrne kicks at
the rubber with new spikes.

Gallagher tells me
not to watch too long.
I have to warm up
our starting pitcher,

a bonus baby
West Point dropout
whose hard one explodes
like a grenade as it
crosses the plate.

But I want to memorize
this grassy field in May sunlight,
the baggy flannel uniforms,
the bald, blunt head of Enos Slaughter
as he grins and signs a ball,
the blonde, nearly bare-breasted woman
interviewing Bob Veale for TV,
her buttocks tense and snug
in grey designer jeans.

I want to memorize
the quizzical expression
on Tommy Byrne's face
as he adjusts his grip
on a batting-practice ball,
the pheasant-brained
radio announcer eating
his fourth hot dog,
the wide-open happiness
of middle-aged baseball players
who never expected this
residue of poise and grace.

It's good to sit here
out of the old timers' way
with my glove in my hands.
When the years have been piled on
and I'm nearer some mortuary,
I'll stand over there, just behind
home plate with the gear on
one last blood-pulsing time.

Pearly Babe

When Babe Ruth died & went to heaven, he was a rookie all over again. His homers & heroics, merely dust motes on a distant moon.

This is a great team, kid, St. Peter told the Babe. You won't be able to crack it for at least another nanosecond.

But the Babe felt good, he was giddy as a lamb, he played catch with a comet & beamed like a Baltimore aureole, happily slapping mustard on a manna-dog & chugging a six-pack of ambrosia.

In less time than it takes to circle the bases of a quark, he made the starting lineup, & as of this writing he's been a superstar—I think it's Betelgeuse—for 22 eternities. Now & then he hits one out of the dark, but whether it's a single, double, triple, or Big Bang is hard to say: up there (or is it in?) they don't keep stats.

Sweet

One lunar eclipse in seven years
and it's raining so we can't see it.
But there's a perfect picture on TV,

over St. Louis, where the Cardinals
play like geniuses against the Braves.
Oh, St. Louis, murmurs Ernie Johnson,

what a sweet franchise. We're in bed,
in Alabama, but I still get
that sliding sensation — planets

riding on the black hip of universe,
the deep shadow of pure night rising
over the pleated lip of Busch Stadium,

and the words *sweet franchise* move
forever outward, like all radio waves,
toward the unreasonable dawn of time —

making chaos sweet, summer endless,
the blue turf fast and true. The ball
coming off the bat makes the most reassuring

sound in the world: the crack of time
straining against the seams,
pouring out toward the warning track.

You're in the outfield now,
dancing under the ball, moonbathing,
the shadow of something — surprise,

a faint smile — crossing over your face.
I can see you now, just counting on
coming back to earth.

KATHRYN DUNN

Question: If You Had Only 24 Hours to Live, What Would You Do?

If I could, I would tell you
all the things I want to do . . . but
the first thing I would do is play baseball
with my kids, my husband pitching,
on a lawn that slopes

treacherously down in right field.
Two young cats wander in and out of the game,
chasing the ball or us, a dog barks
to be let out, and the phone

rings and rings. This first thing I would do
is done at sunset, the light of day stepping
behind thick green trees, and pausing, silently,
for hours, as distant traffic whooshes
through the valley and the sky turns pink
with a shy embarrassment. Batter up:

our daughter belts a line drive
within my husband's pro-ball reach;
he is so proud of her, he misses it gently,
sends me running from centerfield to left,

through the shad bush, deep into juniper,
and I return to see her ponytail wave
as she rounds the bird feeder which marks
third base. And she arrives at home safe —
we are teaching her this, so she will do it
always — and now

her brother is up. I duck behind his father,
who pitches air, no ball, and then he pitches
slow and even, and our son sends it high
overhead, dropping past right field,
rolling toward the woods just like the sun,
and we all run and laugh and argue
about how many invisible runners
have passed our unguarded bases.

Shall I Compare Thee to a Triple Play?

Yes, they cut down the flowers in the outfield, and the flowers
grow again.
A miracle under our feet, every day, every game.
And the power that grows in the green grass
grows in you.

Yes, the infield rests with power.
On the clean dirt and over the base paths
the air is sweet vibrancy.
You are tender and kind and hard when you need to be —
and I really like your thighs —
and this has nothing to do with the baseball poem
except it's true.

Down on the field, the real field with sunlight
and clouds and warmth on the wet grass and
the little flowers that have escaped the mower;
down below us dying bodies are dressed in bright colors;
close your eyes almost shut and they merge with the field;
they leap out of the grass like birds, like dreams
without names or regret.
They move me away from sorrow.
And this, too, is you.

We sing the anthem and the game begins
and I am amazed at your kisses
that are as direct as line drives.
You stretch singles into babies.
You slam doubles off the wall, triples into the alley,
and then as delicate as breath, you place
the bunt where no man can reach it.

Out in the field you know what to do
with the mean hit,
the dying quail,
the low, twisting drive.
. . . and your glove — hmmm — your glove.

Now you hit the ball so hard
that it leaves all gloves, fences, shadows,
cities and gravities. It will
fly, fly away!

Everything is changed.
Nobody can move.
Except the one man,
staggered with joy,
running and running the bases
as long as I live.

Solid Single

There are warm afternoons when light
congeals on the field like honey-colored paint;

when the pitch looms toward the plate big as a pumpkin
and you stand at the back of the box with time enough
to count all one-hundred-and-eight stitches in its rolling seam.

The slow looping swing of the bat is just an afterthought—
its intersecting arc instinctive as breathing.

It's the sound more than the impact that rattles your bones,
that uncomplicated *whack*.

And the horsehide is a small ball again, astonishingly white
as it rockets past short, skims the mitt's web scuffing lace-to-lace,
catches the grass, skips off the nap of the close-clipped turf

as if it were still on the horse, jumping fence
with the faint rub of hooves, sailing into new pastures.

Looking for the Baseball

*Look! Look! If you look really hard at things, you'll forget
you're going to die.*
—Montgomery Clift

*If you cannot find the truth right where you are, where else
do you expect to find it?*
—Dogen

1.

Somewhere out beyond the edge of consciousness
the wild birds are singing, singing
songs of desolation and terror.
Dark horses race across the moon
as I stand in the shadow-dappled snow
at twenty-three below, the air so hard
it hurts to breathe, and even here
the birds are singing, singing,
songs of desolation and terror.

2.

What am I to do with this sudden emptiness
at the core, the frozen heart that will not act,
the waxing bitterness at what this life
will not be? I want to be as pure and cold
and perfect as this winter night, wraiths
of smoke torn by the wind, the wild birds
silenced by the sheer starkness of belief.

What do I believe in? Where are you, God?
Why have you forsaken me, and I you?
That is it finally, isn't it? I am still looking
for God, for faith, for something that gives
meaning beyond this moment. Reading

the obituaries I see the phrase, "Born
this day to eternal life," and I want
to believe that death is just a door, a passing
over into something if not greater then
as good as this life, yet I dare not trust
the goodness of this life, turning ever
to those mad birds singing, and what
are they singing if not my fear of death,
my fear that death is the cold absolute,
the nothing, the less than smoke or shadow.
I want a certainty the intellect cannot provide,
yet have not courage enough to leap
into the absurdity of belief.

3.

Early June, the smell of lilacs still in the air, bridal wreath spilling
across the fence, catnip along the alleyway, the peonies just forming
their dark heads, apple blossoms thick on the backyard trees. Satur-
day morning, fresh-washed sheets snap in the breeze, sweet with the
smell of Tide and spring. How delicious it will be tonight to crawl be-
tween these cool sheets, my hair washed from the ritual of the Satur-
day bath, clean pajamas my mother sewed for Christmas last, falling
asleep in the comfort of these smells, tired from the first Saturday at
the edge of summer vacation, when, freed from the tyranny of clocks,
I will run like the animal I am, free with friends, lost in baseball and
bicycles, fishing, running all day long as if there were only this mo-
ment, the joy of it, nothing else mattering.

A handful of us kicking through the weeds
beyond the edge of the field, looking for
the lost baseball. It does not matter who
hit it, that he ran all the way home, what
matters is there is no game if there is no baseball.
The ball itself has become the color of dirt,
the color of the weeds we part now on hands
and knees. It must be here somewhere. We
retrace the trajectory, walk then beyond

the weeds, into the woods, the flowering quince,
fanning out, insisting we will find it, somewhere.
Dusk calls off the search. I sleep that night
in fresh sheets, dreaming I have found the baseball
in an obvious spot we overlooked. I hold it up,
and joyously we run through sunlight,
sliding into tomorrow because nothing else matters.

4.
We wake to silence as in silence
we fell to sleep, a hundred boys
in bunk beds, thin mattresses, white
sheets, the windows open this
winter night, snow blowing in, feet
on the cold stone floors, sleepwalking
through the dark morning, dressed,
teeth brushed at the communal trough,
face scrubbed, cassock and collar on,
we file into chapel, smells of cornbread
and bacon wafting up from the refectory.

Mass, the Latin give-and-take, a shiver
from the cold or something else, an
ecstasy, God there moving among us,
in my heart, a clarity, lost in the singing,
the rise and fall of chants, the incense,
the blessedness of Christ upon my tongue,
God inside, all a dream, a waking dream,
a shiver down the spine, a certainty.
Here, this is it, this is all. Be.

5.
At Mother's funeral my brothers and I
drank beer in the parking lot, the gray
November day swirling around us,
the wild birds singing then, for the first time

in my heart, singing, this wax figure,
no one I knew, the sickly smell of flowers.

The annual pilgrimage to the grave.
Whose bones are these beneath the ground,
where has that energy, that consciousness
fled, who am I to be standing here, breathing?

6.
That intellect should doubt itself,
is that the beginning of faith again,
that mind should argue for foolishness,
not caring for sense or reason,
is that the way back, and back to what,
the old simple faith, God in his heaven,
angels, too, and the goodly dead
singing his praises while the damned
candle forever in hell? No. Something
else then, a greater faith, and less.

What to make of disbelief, my lost
naiveté, how complicated it's all become,
the sad, doubting intellect, so long
divorced from faith it dare not dream
that, there, in an obvious place,
a place I've looked a hundred times before,
not in the woods, not beneath the flowering quince,
not stuck in some odd depression,
but there at the edge of the field,
right where it should be, the baseball.

LARRY ZIRLIN

Last Baseball Dream of the Season

Although I have no memory
of my career in the majors
my name appears
in the *Baseball Encyclopedia*.
Lifetime average: .241.

Now that you know this dream
you know everything about me.

ACKNOWLEDGMENTS
CONTRIBUTORS

Acknowledgments

CARON ANDREGG: "Solid Single" appears courtesy of the author. Copyright © 2002 by Caron Andregg.

DAVID BAKER: "Cardinals in Spring" and "Supernatural" are reprinted from *Sweet Home, Saturday Night* by permission of the University of Arkansas Press. Copyright © 1991 by David Baker.

JOSEPH BATHANTI: "Softball" first appeared in *Aethlon: The Journal of Sport Literature* (1993). Copyright © 1993 by Joseph Bathanti and used with permission.

RICHARD BEHM: "Looking for the Baseball" first appeared in the *Southern Review* (1996). Copyright © 1996 by Richard Behm and used with permission. "The Origin and Purpose of Baseball" first appeared in *Quarterly West* (1984). Copyright © 1984 by Richard Behm and used with permission.

MICHAEL BLUMENTHAL: "Night Baseball" is reprinted from *Days We Would Rather Know* by Michael Blumenthal (Viking-Penguin, 1984). Copyright © 1984 by Michael Blumenthal and used with permission.

EARL S. BRAGGS: "The Baseball Boys of 1964" is reprinted from *Walking Back from Woodstock* by Earl S. Braggs (Anhinga Press, 1997). Copyright © 1994 by Earl S. Braggs and used with permission.

RICHARD BRAUTIGAN: "A Baseball Game" is reprinted from "The Galilee Hitch-Hiker" in *The Pill Versus the Springhill Mine Disaster*. Copyright © 1965 by Richard Brautigan. Reprinted by permission of Houghton Mifflin Company. All rights reserved.

CHARLES BUKOWSKI: "Betting on the Muse." Copyright © 1996 by

Linda Lee Bukowski. Reprinted from *Betting on the Muse: Poems and Stories* with the permission of Black Sparrow Press.

DAVID CITINO: "Returning to the Field" is reprinted from *The Discipline: New and Selected Poems, 1980–1992* by David Citino (Ohio State University Press, 1992). Copyright © 1992 by David Citino and used with permission.

ROBERT COLLINS: "Catch" is reprinted from *Lives We Have Chosen* by Robert Collins, which won the 1998 Tennessee Chapbook Prize and was published as an interior chapbook in *Poems and Plays* 5. Copyright © 1998 by Robert Collins and used with permission.

TONY COSIER: "Southpaw" first appeared in *Aethlon: The Journal of Sport Literature* (1991). Copyright © 1991 by Tony Cosier and used with permission.

PHILIP DACEY: "America without Baseball" is reprinted from *The Paramour of the Moving Air* by Philip Dacey (*Quarterly Review of Literature* Poetry Book Series, 1999). Copyright © 1999 by Philip Dacey and used with permission.

JIM DANIELS: "Play by Play" is reprinted from *The Long Ball* by Jim Daniels (Pig in a Poke Press, 1988). Copyright © 1988 by Jim Daniels and used with permission. "Polish-American Night, Tiger Stadium" is reprinted from *Blessing the House* by Jim Daniels. Copyright © 1997. Reprinted by permission of the University of Pittsburgh Press.

JOSEPH DUEMER: "Night Baseball in the American West" is reprinted from *Customs* by Joseph Duemer (University of Georgia Press, 1988). Copyright © 1988 by Joseph Duemer and used with permission.

KATHRYN DUNN: "Question: If You Had Only 24 Hours to Live, What Would You Do?" first appeared in *Fan Magazine* (1999). Copyright © 1999 by Kathryn Dunn and used with permission.

KEITH EISNER: "Shall I Compare Thee to a Triple Play?" first appeared in the *Minneapolis Review of Baseball* (1990; now *Elysian Fields Quarterly*). Copyright © 1990 by Keith Eisner and used with permission.

DAVID FEELA: "The Big League" first appeared in *Sport Literate* (1998). Copyright © 1998 by David Feela and used with permission.

BETH ANN FENNELLY: "Asked for a Happy Memory of Her Father, She

Remembers Wrigley Field" first appeared in *Poetry Northwest* (1995). Copyright © 1995 by Beth Ann Fennelly and used with permission.

RINA FERRARELLI: "Crowd at the Stadium" first appeared in *Wind* (1983). Copyright © 1983 by Rina Ferrrarelli and used with permission.

REBECCA J. FINCH: "Ode to Apple Pie" first appeared in *Tar River Poetry* (1996). Copyright © 1996 by Rebecca J. Finch and used with permission.

GARY FINCKE: "The Career of Lou Proctor" appears courtesy of the author. Copyright © 2002 by Gary Fincke.

ROBERT GIBB: "Listening to the Ballgame" is reprinted from *Momentary Days* by Robert Gibb (Walt Whitman Cultural Arts Center, 1989). Copyright © 1989 by Robert Gibb and used with permission. "Williams in Autumn" is reprinted from *Fugue for a Late Snow* by Robert Gibb, by permission of the University of Missouri Press. Copyright © 1993 by the Curators of the University of Missouri.

LAURENCE GOLDSTEIN: "Is Reality One or Many?" is reprinted from *Cold Reading* by Laurence Goldstein (Copper Beech Press, 1995). Copyright © 1995 by Laurence Goldstein and used with permission.

JOSEPH GREEN: "The Catch" appeared in *Willow Springs* (1996). Copyright © 1996 by Joseph Green and used with permission.

LINDA GREGERSON: "Line Drive Caught by the Grace of God" is reprinted from *The Woman Who Died in Her Sleep* by Linda Gregerson. Copyright © 1996 by Linda Gregerson. Reprinted by permission of Houghton Mifflin Company. All rights reserved.

LOUISE GRIECO: "It Ain't Over . . ." appears courtesy of the author. Copyright © 1997 by Louise Grieco.

PAUL R. HAENEL: "Short History of a Baseball" appears courtesy of the author. Copyright © 2002 by Paul R. Haenel.

KATHERINE HARER: "The Cure" appears courtesy of the author. Copyright © 2002 by Katherine Harer.

MICHAEL S. HARPER: "Archives" is reprinted from *Honorable Amendments* by Michael S. Harper (University of Illinois Press, 1995). Copyright © 1995 by Michael S. Harper and used with permission.

MARY KENNAN HERBERT: "Night Baseball, 1947" first appeared in *Fan*

Magazine (1996). Copyright © 1996 by Mary Kennan Herbert and used with permission.

WILLIAM HEYEN: "If You Know Me at All" is from *The Host: Selected Poems 1965–1990* by William Heyen. Reprinted by permission of Time Being Books. Copyright © 1994 by Time Being Press. All rights reserved.

CONRAD HILBERRY: "Stop Action" is reprinted from *The Moon Seen as a Slice of Pineapple* by Conrad Hilberry (University of Georgia Press, 1984). Copyright © 1984 by Conrad Hilberry and used with permission.

MIKHAIL HOROWITZ: "Pearly Babe" first appeared in *Elysian Fields Quarterly* (1999). Copyright © 1999 by Mikhail Horowitz and used with permission.

ANDREW HUDGINS: "In the Red Seats" is reprinted from *Babylon in a Jar*. Copyright © 1998 by Andrew Hudgins. Reprinted by permission of Houghton Mifflin Company. All rights reserved.

DAVID JAUSS: "How to Hit a Home Run" first appeared in *Poetry Now* (1979). Copyright © 1979 by David Jauss and used with permission.

MICHELLE JONES: "My Father, on the Day He Died" first appeared in *Elysian Fields Quarterly* (1993). Copyright © 1993 by Michelle Jones and used with permission.

KAREN KEVORKIAN: "Softball Dreams" first appeared in the *Massachusetts Review* (1983). Copyright © 1983 by Karen Kevorkian and used with permission.

LINDSAY KNOWLTON: "Sweet Spot" appears courtesy of the author. Copyright © 1997 by Lindsay Knowlton.

YUSEF KOMUNYAKAA: "Glory" is reprinted from *Magic City* by Yusef Komunyakaa (Wesleyan University Press, 1992). Copyright © 1992 by Yusef Komunyakaa. Reprinted by permission of Wesleyan University Press.

NORBERT KRAPF: "Dream of a Hanging Curve" is reprinted from *Country* by Norbert Krapf (Archer Books, 2002). Copyright © 1999 by Norbert Krapf and used with permission.

DONNA J. GELAGOTIS LEE: "Winter at the Ball Field" and "Final Play" first appeared in *Fan Magazine* (1998). Copyright © 1998 by Donna J. Gelagotis Lee and used with permission.

JOEL LEWIS: "A Dharma Talk by Johnny Roseboro, Boulder, Colorado,

March 23, 1983" first appeared in *Hanging Loose* 57 (1990). Copyright © 1990 by Joel Lewis and used with permission.

M. L. LIEBLER: "Instant Out" appears courtesy of the author. Copyright © 1997 by M. L. Liebler.

GEORGE LOONEY: "Tired of Loss and Sin" appears courtesy of the author. Copyright © 2002 by George Looney.

PAUL MARION: "Spring Fever" is reprinted from *Strong Place: Poems '74–'84* by Paul Marion (Loom Press, 1984). Copyright © 1984 by Paul Marion and used with permission.

ED MARKOWSKI: "My Last Hit" first appeared in *Fan Magazine* (1999). Copyright © 1999 by Ed Markowski and used with permission.

THOMAS MICHAEL MCDADE: "Players" first appeared in *Nerve Cowboy* (1999). Copyright © 1999 by Thomas Michael McDade and used with permission.

WALT MCDONALD: "Where Baseball's the Only Game in Town" first appeared in *Black Fly Review* (1990). Copyright © 1990 by Walt McDonald and used with permission.

ROBERT MCDOWELL: "The Gamer" first appeared in *Harvard Magazine* 91.2 (November/December 1988). Copyright © 1988 by Robert McDowell and used with permission.

RON MCFARLAND: "Photo of a Minor League Baseball Team, ca. 1952" is reprinted from *Ballgloves* by Ron McFarland (Polo Grounds Press, 2000). Copyright © 1993 by Ron McFarland and used with permission. "Why I Love Baseball" is reprinted with the permission of Confluence Press from *Stranger in Town* by Ron McFarland. Copyright © 2000 by Ron McFarland.

MICHAEL MCFEE: "Baseball Fields Seen from the Air" and "Old Baseball Found under a Bush" are reprinted from Michael McFee: *Colander* by permission of Carnegie Mellon University Press. Copyright © 1996 by Michael McFee.

WESLEY MCNAIR: "The Retarded Children Play Baseball" is reprinted from *Talking in the Dark* by Wesley McNair. Reprinted by permission of David R. Godine, Publishers, Inc. Copyright © 1998 by Wesley McNair.

JAY MEEK: "Visiting My Boyhood Friend after His Stroke" is reprinted from Jay Meek: *Trains in Winter* by permission of Carnegie Mellon University Press. Copyright © 2002 by Jay Meek.

Acknowledgments

PETER MEINKE: "A Dream of Third Base" is from *Night Watch on the Chesapeake* by Peter Meinke, copyright © 1987. Reprinted by permission of the University of Pittsburgh Press.

BILL MEISSNER: "Something about Certain Old Baseball Fields" first appeared in *Midwest Quarterly* (1995). Copyright © 1995 by Bill Meissner and used with permission.

MARK J. MITCHELL: "Minor League Rainout, Iowa" first appeared in *Fan Magazine* (1997). Copyright © 1997 by Mark J. Mitchell and used with permission.

ELINOR NAUEN: "Spring Training" is reprinted from *American Guys*, copyright © 1997 by Elinor Nauen, by permission of Hanging Loose Press and the author.

J. CAITLIN OAKES: "Baseball" first appeared in *Willow Springs* (1996). Copyright © 1996 by J. Caitlain Oakes and used with permission.

GAILMARIE PAHMEIER: "Telephone Call" copyright © 1990 by Gailmarie Pahmeier. From *The House on Breakaheart Road* by Gailmarie Pahmeier. Reprinted with the permission of the University of Nevada Press.

CRAIG PAULENICH: "To Fungo the Torn Ones" first appeared in *Tar River Poetry* (1999). Copyright © 1999 by Craig Paulenich and used with permission.

CAROL J. PIERMAN: "Sweet" first appeared in *Sycamore Review* (1992). Copyright © 1992 by Carol J. Pierman and used with permission.

JOHN C. PINE: "Black Ink" is reprinted from *Cliff Walk* by John C. Pine (Moveable Feast Press, 1985). Copyright © 1985 by John C. Pine and used with permission.

WYATT PRUNTY: "Baseball" is reprinted from the *The Run of the House*. Copyright © 1993. The Johns Hopkins University Press.

DAN QUISENBERRY: "Baseball Cards" is reprinted from *On Days Like This* by Dan Quisenberry (Helicon Nine Editions, 1998). Copyright © 1998 by the Estate of Dan Quisenberry. Reprinted by permission of Helicon Nine Editions.

MAJ RAGAIN: "Blyleven's Fourth Shutout, June, 1985" is reprinted from *Burley One Dark Sucker Fired* (Bottom Dog Press, 1998). Copyright © 1998 by Bottom Dog Press/Maj Ragain and used with permission.

DALE RITTERBUSCH: "World Series, 1968, Southeast Asia" first appeared in *War, Literature and the Arts: An International Journal of the Humanities* (1998). Copyright © 1998 by Dale Ritterbusch and used with permission.

JAY ROGOFF: "Aesthetics" and "Everything But Everything" are reprinted from *The Cutoff* by Jay Rogoff (The Word Works, 1995). Copyright © 1995 by Jay Rogoff and used with permission.

EDWIN ROMOND: "Something I Could Tell You about Love" is reprinted from *Home Fire* by Edwin Romond (Belle Mead Press, 1993). Copyright © 1993 by Edwin Romond and used with permission.

VIRGINIA SCHAEFER: "Baseball in Ohio" appears courtesy of the author. Copyright © 2002 by Virginia Schaefer.

MARK W. SCHRAF: "Question and Answer" is reprinted from *I Saw Rod Scurry* by Mark W. Schraf (Polo Grounds Press, 1997). Copyright © 1997 by Mark W. Schraf and used with permission.

RED SHUTTLEWORTH: "Carolina League Old Timers Game" first appeared in the *Minneapolis Review of Baseball* (1985; now *Elysian Fields Quarterly*). Copyright © 1985 by Red Shuttleworth and used with permission.

JOYCE SIDMAN: "The Player" first appeared in *Fan Magazine* (1995). Copyright © 1995 by Joyce Sidman and used with permission.

FLOYD SKLOOT: "Voices of the Sea" is reprinted from *Music Appreciation* by Floyd Skloot (University Press of Florida, 1994). Copyright © 1994 by Floyd Skloot and reprinted with the permission of the University Press of Florida.

JOSEPH A. SOLDATI: "1947" is reprinted from *Making My Name* by Joseph A. Soldati (Mellen Poetry Press, 1992). Copyright © 1992 by Joseph A. Soldati and used with permission.

JOSEPH STANTON: "Stealing Home" first appeared in *Elysian Fields Quarterly* (1999). Copyright © 1999 by Joseph Stanton and used with permission.

DAVID STARKEY: "September Pears" first appeared in *Connecticut River Review* (1994). Copyright © 1994 by David Starkey and used with permission.

SHERYL ST. GERMAIN: "A Softball Game" first appeared in *The Journals of Scheherazade* by Sheryl St. Germain (University of North Texas

Press, 1996). Copyright © 1996 by Sheryl St. Germain and used with permission.

RODNEY TORRESON: "Dreams Should Not Dog Great Center Fielders" is reprinted from *The Ripening of Pinstripes* by Rodney Torreson (Story Line Press, 1998). Copyright © 1998 by Rodney Torreson and used with permission.

QUINCY TROUPE: "Poem for My Father" is reprinted from *Avalanche* (Coffee House Press, 1996). Copyright © 1996 by Quincy Troupe and used with permission.

RON VAZZANO: "Baseball Haiku" appears courtesy of the author. Copyright © 2002 by Ron Vazzano.

CONSTANTINE VON HOFFMAN: "Geronimo at Short" appears courtesy of the author. Copyright © 2002 by Constantine von Hoffman.

DOYLE WESLEY WALLS: "Hits" first appeared in *Spitball: The Literary Baseball Magazine* (1995). Copyright © 1995 by Doyle Wesley Walls and used with permission.

DAVID C. WARD: "Isn't it pretty to think so?" first appeared in *Aethlon: The Journal of Sport Literature* (1999). Copyright © 1999 by David C. Ward and used with permission.

EDWARD R. WARD: "Limited Power" is reprinted from *Where Memory Gathers: Baseball and Poetry* by Edward R. Ward (Rudi Publishing, 1998). Copyright © 1998 by Edward R. Ward and used with permission.

MICHAEL WATERS: "Singles" is reprinted from Michael Waters: *Anniversary of the Air* by permission of Carnegie Mellon University Press. Copyright © 1985 by Michael Waters. Copyright © 2001 by Michael Waters. Reprinted from *Parthenopi: New and Selected Poems*, by Michael Waters, with the permission of BOA Editions, Ltd.

DAVID WATTS: "Little League Tryouts" first appeared in the *Gettysburg Review* 5.3 and is reprinted here with the acknowledgment of the editors. Copyright © 1992 by David Watts and used with permission.

KYLE LEE WILLIAMS: "True Story" first appeared in *Fan Magazine* (1999). Copyright © 1999 by Kyle Lee Williams and used with permission.

HANNAH WILSON: "October Play" first appeared in *Elysian Fields Quarterly* (1998). Copyright © 1998 by Hannah Wilson and used with permission.

JEFF WORLEY: "Biographical Note" first appeared in *Mid-American Review* (1987). Copyright © 1987 by Jeff Worley and used with permission.

BARON WORMSER: "Listening to a Baseball Game" is reprinted from *When,* by Baron Wormser, published by Sarabande Books, Inc. Copyright © 1997 by Baron Wormser. Reprinted by permission of Sarabande Books and the author.

KAREN ZABOROWSKI: "World Series, Game 5" first appeared in the *Paterson Literary Review* 26 (1997). Copyright © 1997 by Karen Zaborowski and used with permission.

LARRY ZIRLIN: "Last Baseball Dream of the Season" appears courtesy of the author. Copyright © 2002 by Larry Zirlin.

Contributors

CARON ANDREGG lives and writes in San Diego County with her husband and several dogs, cats, and sundry other animals. Her poems have appeared in *Spillway, Rattle, Poetry International, Solo,* and other journals. She is also the publisher and coeditor of *Cider Press Review.*

DAVID BAKER is the author of eight books, including *Changeable Thunder* (poems, 2001) and *Heresy and the Ideal* (criticism, 2000). He teaches at Denison University and in the MFA program at Warren Wilson College. He is poetry editor of the *Kenyon Review.*

JOSEPH BATHANTI teaches English and is writer-in-residence at Mitchell College in Statesville, North Carolina. His most recent book of poems, *This Metal,* won the Oscar Arnold Young Award. His novel, *East Liberty,* winner of the Carolina Novel Award, was published in October 2001.

RICHARD BEHM is a professor of English at the University of Wisconsin-Stevens Point. His poems have been published in the *Sewanee Review,* the *Kenyon Review,* the *Southern Review, Michigan Quarterly Review,* and many other journals.

MICHAEL BLUMENTHAL is a novelist, poet, essayist, and translator whose memoir *So Many Fathers and Mothers* will be published by HarperCollins in 2002. He only wishes, as does his son, he had been as good a baseball player as the poem included herein suggests.

EARL S. BRAGGS is an associate professor of English at the University of Tennessee at Chattanooga. He is the author of *Hat Dancer Blue, Walking Back From Woodstock,* and *House on Fontanka.* A chapter,

"After Allyson," from his novel in progress won the 1995 Jack Kerouac Literary Prize.

RICHARD BRAUTIGAN authored twenty-three books of poetry and fiction, including *Trout Fishing in America* and *The Pill Versus the Springhill Mine Disaster*. An iconic writer who emerged during the Beat Generation and became synonymous with 1960s youth culture, Brautigan has been described by Guy Davenport as "a kind of Thoreau who cannot keep a straight face." He died in 1984 of an apparently self-inflicted gunshot wound.

CHARLES BUKOWSKI was a prolific writer of poetry and fiction. His poetry alone amounts to more than fifty books, including *It Catches My Heart in Its Hands: New and Selected Poems, 1955–1963*, and *Love Is a Dog from Hell: Poems, 1974–1977*. In addition to seven novels and six short story collections, he authored more than twenty other works, ranging from collections of letters to an autobiographical screenplay for the movie *Barfly*, released in 1987. He died of leukemia in 1994.

DAVID CITINO is a professor of English and creative writing at Ohio State University. He is the author of twelve books of poetry, including *The Gift of Fire*, *The Invention of Secrecy*, *The Book of Appassionata: Collected Poems*, and *Broken Symmetry*, named a Notable Book of 1997 by the National Book Critics Circle. He writes on poetry for the *Columbus Dispatch* and is contributing editor of a book of prose, *The Eye of the Poet* (Oxford University Press).

ROBERT COLLINS has published three chapbooks, *The Inventor Poems*, *The Glass Blower*, and *Lives We Have Chosen*. His poems have appeared in many journals and magazines. He directs the creative writing program at the University of Alabama at Birmingham, where he also teaches American literature and poetry writing and edits *Birmingham Poetry Review*.

TONY COSIER, a Canadian author, coaches soccer and teaches high school English in Ottawa. His most recent collection of verse is *Clearwater Tarn*, published by Penumbra Press.

PHILIP DACEY's sixth and seventh books appeared in 1999: *The Deathbed Playboy* (Eastern Washington University Press) and *The Paramour of the Moving Air* (Quarterly Review of Literature). As a young

St. Louis Browns fan, Dacey saw Eddie Gaedel, the midget briefly an employee of Bill Veeck, draw a walk.

JIM DANIELS's most recent books include *City Pool* (New Issues Press, 2002), *Blue Jesus* (Carnegie Mellon University Press, 2000), and *No Pets* (Bottom Dog Press, 1999).

JOSEPH DUEMER's most recent book is *Magical Thinking* (Ohio State University Press, 2001). In 2000–2001, he was a Fulbright fellow in Hanoi, Vietnam. He teaches at Clarkson University in northern New York.

KATHRYN DUNN leads creative writing workshops for adults and teens. Her work has appeared in *Peregrine*, the *Minnesota Review*, *Exquisite Corpse*, *Fan*, and *Yankee Magazine*. She lives with her husband and two children in western Massachusetts.

KEITH EISNER is an actor in Olympia, Washington. When he can, he listens to the Mariners backstage. He wrote the poem included in this collection for his wife, Marty.

DAVID FEELA teaches at Montezuma-Cortez High School in Cortez, Colorado, and writes poems and essays from his corner of the Four Corners. His website: www.geocities.com/feelasophy.

BETH ANN FENNELLY is from Chicago and teaches English at Knox College in Galesburg, Illinois. She was the 1998–99 Diane Middlebrook fellow at the University of Wisconsin. Her poems have been anthologized in *The Pushcart Prize 2001*, *The Penguin Book of the Sonnet*, and *The Best American Poetry 1996*.

RINA FERRARELLI has published a book and a chapbook of original poetry, *Home is a Foreign Country* (Eadmer Press, 1996) and *Dreamsearch* (Malafemmina Press, 1992), and two books of translated poetry. She has been awarded a National Endowment for the Arts Literature Fellowship in Translation for poetry and the Italo Calvino Prize from the Columbia University Translation Center.

REBECCA J. FINCH lives on a blueberry farm ten miles from Five County Stadium, home of the Carolina Mudcats. She is current president of the Poetry Council of North Carolina. Her poems have been published in periodicals and several anthologies.

GARY FINCKE is the director of the Writer's Institute at Susquehanna University. His most recent books are *Blood Ties* (Time Being Books, 2001) and *The Almanac for Desire* (BkMk Press, 2000).

ROBERT GIBB's most recent collection, *The Origins of Evening*, was a National Poetry Series winner. Other awards include a National Endowment for the Arts Poetry Fellowship, a Pushcart Prize, the Wildwood Prize in Poetry, and the Camden Poetry Award.

LAURENCE GOLDSTEIN is the author of three books of poetry, most recently *Cold Reading* (Copper Beech Press, 1995), and three books of literary criticism, most recently *The American Poet at the Movies: A Critical History* (University of Michigan Press, 1994). He is professor of English at the University of Michigan, where he has edited *Michigan Quarterly Review* since 1977.

JOSEPH GREEN was PEN Northwest's Margery Davis Boyden Wilderness Writer for 2000. He Lives in Longview, Washington, and teaches at Lower Columbia College. A collection of his poems, *Deluxe Motel*, is available from the Signpost Press at Western Washington University.

LINDA GREGERSON's most recent book is *The Woman Who Died in Her Sleep* (Houghton Mifflin, 1996). Her most recent book of criticism is *Negative Capability: Contemporary American Poetry* (University of Michigan Press, 2001). She teaches Renaissance literature and creative writing at the University of Michigan.

LOUISE GRIECO has published poems in a number of small press magazines, most recently *Thirteenth Moon* (SUNY-Albany). She lives and writes in Albany, New York, and works for a public library.

PAUL R. HAENEL, a native of Pittsburgh, Pennsylvania, published his first volume of poems, *Farewell, Goodbye, Wave Goodbye*, in 1994 with Washington Writers Publishing House. He lives in Alexandria, Virginia, and has worked at Morgan Stanley for too many years to mention.

KATHERINE HARER is the author of four books of poetry. She teaches at Skyline Community College just south of San Francisco. She is currently finishing work on a book of interviews with pro baseball players across the generations and beginning a new book of conversations with women in pro ball.

MICHAEL S. HARPER, the poet laureate of Rhode Island, has authored ten books of poetry, most recently 1995's *Honorable Amendments*. He has edited or compiled an additional five titles, most recently *The Vintage Book of African American Poetry* (2000). He is a mem-

ber of the American Academy of Arts and Letters, as well as the
American Academy of Arts and Sciences. He is University Profes-
sor of English at Brown University, where he directs the writing
program.

MARY KENNAN HERBERT teaches writing and literature at colleges in
New York City. Her poems have appeared in numerous literary
journals in print and on the web in thirteen different countries. Her
first three books of poetry were published by Ginninderra Press
in Australia, and her fourth collection was published in December
2000 by Meadow Geese Press in Massachusetts.

WILLIAM HEYEN retired in 2000 as SUNY-Brockport's poet-in-residence.
His books include *Erika: Poems of the Holocaust, The Host: Selected
Poems, Pig Notes and Dumb Music: Prose on Poetry* (containing his
baseball essay "Stats"), and *Crazy Horse in Stillness*, winner of 1997's
Small Press Book Award for Poetry.

CONRAD HILBERRY has taught for many years at Kalamazoo College in
Michigan. His most recent books are *Player Piano* (poems, Louisi-
ana State University Press, 1999), *Taking Notes on Nature's Wild In-
ventions* (poems, Snowy Egret, 1999), and *Sorting the Smoke* (new
and selected poems, University of Iowa Press, 1990).

MIKHAIL HOROWITZ, a Hudson Valley performance poet who edits
books at Total Sports, is the author of *Big League Poets* (City Lights,
1978), a compendium of collages and captions recapitulating the
baseball careers of such immortals as Whitey Whitman and Smokey
Coleridge.

ANDREW HUDGINS is Distinguished Research Professor of English at
the University of Cincinnati. He has published five books of po-
etry, all with Houghton Mifflin. The most recent is *Babylon in a Jar*
(1999). His collection of essays, *The Glass Anvil*, was published by
the University of Michigan Press in 1997. His memories of baseball
consist of his standing anxiously in right field while various adults
screamed at him.

DAVID JAUSS teaches at the University of Arkansas at Little Rock and in
the Vermont College MFA program. His most recent books are *Im-
provising Rivers*, a collection of poems, and *Black Maps*, a collec-
tion of stories.

MICHELLE JONES taught twentieth-century American and British literature and gender studies at Muskingum College in Ohio for ten years. She recently accepted an appointment with the U.S. Department of State, working at the U.S. embassy in Warsaw. Like her late father, she was born and will die a Tigers fan. She has a son and a daughter.

KAREN KEVORKIAN's poems and stories have appeared in *Antioch Review, Massachusetts Quarterly Review, Virginia Quarterly Review, Third Coast,* and *Hambone.* Her fiction has appeared in *Fiction International, Mississippi Review,* and *Five Fingers Review.* She is an art-book editor in San Francisco.

LINDSAY KNOWLTON lives in Vermont and received her MFA from Warren Wilson College. She has been a fellow twice at the MacDowell Colony, is an avid birder, and likes to walk.

YUSEF KOMUNYAKAA, originally from Bogalusa, Louisiana, has three new books: *Blue Notes: Essays, Interviews, and Commentaries* (University of Michigan Press), *Talking Dirty to the Gods* (poems, Farrar, Straus and Giroux), and *Pleasure Dome: New and Collected Poems, 1975–1999* (Wesleyan). Among his other titles are *Thieves of Paradise,* a finalist for the 1999 National Book Critics Circle Award; *Neon Vernacular: New and Selected Poems 1977–1989,* winner of the 1994 Pulitzer Prize; *Magic City;* and *Dien Cai Dau.*

NORBERT KRAPF, a native of southern Indiana, has published sports poems in his *Somewhere in Southern Indiana* (1993) and *The Country I Come From* (2002), which includes "Dream of a Hanging Curve." He directs the C. W. Post Poetry Center of Long Island University.

DONNA J. GELAGOTIS LEE has poetry published or forthcoming in *The Bitter Oleander, CALYX Journal,* the *Cortland Review, Fan, Hurricane Alice,* the *Midwest Quarterly, Modern Haiku,* and *Wisconsin Review.* She is a freelance editor in Princeton, New Jersey.

JOEL LEWIS is the author of *Vertical's Currency: New and Selected Poems* (Talisman House). He daydreams about the great marginal baseball heroes of his youth in the mid 1960s and early 1970s: Smokey Burgess, Hoyt Wilhelm and the Designated Hebrew himself, Ron "Boomer" Blomberg.

M. L. LIEBLER is the author of *Written in Rain: New and Selected Poems* (Tebot Bach, 2000), *Breaking the Voodoo and Other Poems* (Adastra, 2001), and several CDs of music and poetry, including *Paper Ghost*

Rain Dance (2001) with The Magic Poetry Band and *Voodoo Break* (2001) with Country Joe McDonald. He teaches literature, creative writing, and labor studies at Wayne State University and is the Detroit director of the YMCA National Writer's Voice Project.

GEORGE LOONEY's second book, *Attendant Ghosts*, was published by Cleveland State University Press in 2000. His first, *Animals Housed in the Pleasure of Flesh*, won the 1995 Bluestem Award. He teaches creative writing at Penn State-Erie.

PAUL MARION is the author of several collections of poetry. He is also the editor of a collection of Jack Kerouac works, *Atop an Underwood: Early Stories and Other Writings*. He lives in Lowell, Massachusetts.

ED MARKOWSKI is a mental-health counselor and poet who resides in Auburn Hills, Michigan, with his wife. His work has been featured on Detroit Public Radio and has appeared in *Fan, The Poetry Motel, City Magazine*, and the *Birmingham Poetry Review*.

THOMAS MICHAEL MCDADE lives in Monroe, Connecticut, with his wife and works as a computer programmer in the plumbing industry. His work has recently been published in *Aethlon* and *Elysian Fields Quarterly*.

WALT MCDONALD, a former Air Force pilot, has published nineteen collections of poetry and fiction including *All Occasions* (Notre Dame, 2000). Four of his books have won awards from the National Cowboy Hall of Fame.

ROBERT MCDOWELL's *Islanders All* will be published in the Pitt Poetry Series, University of Pittsburgh Press, in April 2002. He is an eight-year player-manager in two Oregon Men's Senior Baseball Leagues (lifetime average: .338).

RON MCFARLAND teaches seventeenth-century and modern poetry, contemporary Northwest writers, the works of Hemingway, and creative writing at the University of Idaho. His new and selected poems, *Stranger in Town* (Confluence Press), and his baseball chapbook, *Ballgloves* (Polo Grounds Press), were both published in the fall of 2000.

MICHAEL MCFEE has published six books of poetry, most recently *Earthly* and *Colander*, both from Carnegie Mellon University Press. He teaches at the University of North Carolina-Chapel Hill and lives in Durham, where his poems have appeared in *Bulls Illustrated: The Official Magazine of the Durham Bulls*.

WESLEY MCNAIR has received grants from the Rockefeller, Fulbright, and Guggenheim foundations, as well as two National Endowment for the Arts Fellowships for creative writers. He has won prizes in poetry from *Poetry*, *Poetry Northwest*, and *Yankee* and has published seven collections.

JAY MEEK's work includes seven collections of poetry, most recently *Trains in Winter* (Carnegie Mellon University Press, 2002), and a novel, *The Memphis Letters* (also published by Carnegie Mellon, 2000). He teaches at the University of North Dakota.

PETER MEINKE has published twelve books of poetry, six in the Pitt Poetry Series, the most recent being *Zinc Fingers*, which received the 2001 Southeast Booksellers Association Award. He lives in St. Petersburg, home of the hapless Devil Rays.

BILL MEISSNER's book of baseball short fiction, *Hitting into the Wind*, is available in paperback from Southern Methodist University Press. Meissner is the director of creative writing at St. Cloud State University in Minnesota, and he plays baseball with a group he calls the Catch and Release Baseball Club.

MARK J. MITCHELL, a widely published poet, now also finds himself a struggling novelist. He grew up on the Dodgers of Sandy Koufax and Don Drysdale but underwent a midlife conversion to the Giants. This makes his wife, filmmaker Joan Juster, very proud.

ELINOR NAUEN edited *Diamonds Are a Girl's Best Friend: Women Writers on Baseball* (Faber and Faber, 1994), and her baseball writing has appeared in *Up Late: American Poetry since 1970*, *Cult Baseball Players*, *Baseball Diary*, *Elysian Fields Quarterly*, *Aethlon* and *Nine*. She once threw out the first pitch (a strike) at a St. Paul, Minnesota, Saints game.

J. CAITLIN OAKES grew up in Minnesota and watched as the Twins' perfect, open-air field became the Metrodome, which changed the whole nature of the game by removing the sky as a factor. Oakes now lives and writes in Walla Walla, Washington. Her poems have appeared in the *Paris Review*, *Poetry East*, *Poetry Northwest*, and other journals.

GAILMARIE PAHMEIER teaches creative writing workshops and contemporary literature courses at the University of Nevada. Widely anthologized, she is the author of three collections of poetry, including *The House on Breakaheart Road*.

CRAIG PAULENICH is an associate professor of English and writing coordinator at Kent State University-Salem. He was the recipient of the Academy of American Poets Award at the University of Pittsburgh in 1982. His poems have appeared in the *Georgia Review, Kansas Review, South Carolina Review, Southern Poetry Review, Tar River Poetry*, and *Windhorse*.

CAROL J. PIERMAN is a 2001 recipient of an Alabama Council on the Arts fellowship. Her books include *The Age of Krypton* (Carnegie Mellon University Press) and *The Naturalized Citizen* (New Rivers). She is on the faculty of the University of Alabama and is currently at work on a study of the All-American Girls Professional Baseball League and its Players Association.

JOHN C. PINE was born in New York City in 1922. He is the author of five books of poetry, including *Still Alive*, published in 2000. His poem "Cardinals" was nominated for a Pushcart Prize by White Eagle Coffee Store Press in 1996. He lives in El Dorado Hills, California.

WYATT PRUNTY is the director of the Sewanee Writers' Conference and Carlton Professor of English at the University of the South. He is the author of seven books of poetry, including *Unarmed and Dangerous: New and Selected Poems* (Johns Hopkins University Press). His critical work *"Fallen from the Symboled World": Precedents for the New Formalism* is available from Oxford University Press. He is the general editor of the Sewanee Writers' Series, published by Sewanee in conjunction with The Overlook Press.

DAN QUISENBERRY's poems have appeared in *Aethlon, Fan, Thorny Locust, Spitball*, and *New Letters*. He published the chapbook *Down and In* and the collection *On Days Like This* (Helicon Nine Editions). In twelve seasons of major-league baseball, Quisenberry racked up 244 saves and posted a 2.76 e.r.a. His Kansas City Royals won two pennants and the 1985 World Series. Roger Angell on Quisenberry: "Like his pitches, Dan Quisenberry's poems come at you unexpectedly . . . startling you with a late swoop or slant:

What was *that?*" Quisenberry died of a brain tumor in 1998 at age forty-five.

MAJ RAGAIN has hosted the open poetry readings at Brady's Cafe, Kent, Ohio, since 1983 and teaches creative writing at Kent State University. A fourth collection of poems, *Twist the Axe*, was published by Bottom Dog Press in 2001.

DALE RITTERBUSCH is the author of *Lessons Learned*, a collection of poems on the Vietnam War and its aftermath. He is an associate professor of languages and literatures at the University of Wisconsin-Whitewater.

JAY ROGOFF's Washington Prize–winning book of poems, *The Cutoff* (Word Works, 1995), takes place in the world of minor-league ball. His poetry and criticism appear regularly in such journals as the *Georgia Review*, the *Kenyon Review*, and *Salmagundi*.

EDWIN ROMOND lives in Wind Gap, Pennsylvania, with his wife and son. He is the author of two books of poetry: *Home Fire* and *Macaroons*, and his dream is to become the poet laureate of the New York Yankees.

VIRGINIA SCHAEFER teaches writing and literature at Kent State University-Stark.

MARK W. SCHRAF is the fiction editor of *Spitball* and staff sports writer for *West Virginia Family Magazine*. His chapbook of baseball poems, *I Saw Rod Scurry*, was published by Polo Grounds Press in 1997, and McFarland published *Cooperstown Verses and Voices: Poems about Baseball's Hall of Famers* in 2001.

RED SHUTTLEWORTH, recently retired Big Bend Community College assistant baseball coach and 1980 bullpen coach for the Durham Bulls, is the author of twenty-seven produced plays and a recent book of poems from University of Nevada Press, *Western Settings*.

JOYCE SIDMAN won the 1999 New Women's Voices Award for her book *Like the Air* (Finishing Line Press). Her latest book, *Wizards: Poems about Inventors* (Millbrook), is for teenagers. She spent many summer twilights watching her sons play ball.

FLOYD SKLOOT's most recent collections of poetry are *The Evening Light* (Story Line Press, 2001) and *The Fiddler's Trance* (Bucknell University Press, 2001). His essay about the healing powers of baseball trivia appeared in *The Best American Essays 1993*.

JOSEPH A. SOLDATI of Portland, Oregon, an outstanding sandlot player in his youth, is an emeritus professor of English at Western Oregon University and the author of two poetry collections. He has published poems and essays in numerous literary journals and magazines.

JOSEPH STANTON's poems have appeared in *Poetry, Harvard Review, Elysian Fields Quarterly, Aethlon,* and numerous other journals. His books of poems include *Imaginary Museum* (Time Being Books, 1999) and a volume of baseball poems forthcoming from McFarland. He teaches art history and American studies at the University of Hawai'i at Manoa.

DAVID STARKEY teaches creative writing at North Central College and is the editor of *Teaching Writing Creatively* (Heinemann-Boynton/ Cook, 1998) and coeditor of *Smokestacks and Skyscrapers: An Anthology of Chicago Literature* (Loyola, 1999). He has published several collections of poems including *Koan Americana, Adventures of the Minor Poet, A Year with Gayle,* and *Open Mike Night at the Cabaret Voltaire.*

SHERYL ST. GERMAIN, originally from New Orleans, teaches creative writing at Iowa State University. Her books include *Going Home, The Mask of Medusa, Making Bread at Midnight, How Heavy the Breath of God,* and *The Journals of Scheherazade.* She has published a book of translations of the Cajun poet Jean Arceneaux, *Je Suis Cadien.*

RODNEY TORRESON's poems have appeared in a wide range of journals and anthologies, including *The Third Coast, Passages North,* and *Hummers, Knucklers, and Slow Curves.* He lives and teaches in Grand Rapids, Michigan.

QUINCY TROUPE, whose father, Quincy Trouppe, played and managed in the Negro Leagues from 1930 to 1949, is the author or editor of thirteen books. He has received two American Book Awards: in 1980 for poetry for *Snake-Back Solos* and in 1990 for *Miles: The Autobiography* (cowritten with Miles Davis). He is a professor of creative writing and American and Caribbean literature at the University of California-San Diego.

RON VAZZANO's poetry has appeared in *Spitball, Fan,* the *New Renaissance, Santa Barbara Review, Thema, Bone and Flesh, Prairie*

Winds, and elsewhere. He was nominated for a Pushcart Prize in 1997 and has won first place in Internet poetry contests sponsored by Hugo Boss and America Online.

CONSTANTINE VON HOFFMAN was born in Chicago, where he was one of the few Cubs fans on the South Side. He moved to Providence, Rhode Island, at age eight, where he became a Red Sox fan. He hates the Mets and the phrase "lovable losers" with equal passion. A longtime journalist, he currently makes his living as a freelance writer.

DOYLE WESLEY WALLS has published poems in *New York Quarterly*, *Poet and Critic*, the *Minnesota Review*, *Puerto del Sol*, and the *Beloit Poetry Review*. He has also published personal essays, fiction, cartoons, literary criticism, and pedagogical essays. He is the chair of the English department at Pacific University in Forest Grove, Oregon.

DAVID C. WARD is a historian at the Smithsonian Institution and a poet whose work has appeared in many American and English magazines.

EDWARD R. WARD is a Catholic priest (Carmelite Order). He was born in Joliet, Illinois, and raised on the Chicago White Sox. He is the author of *Where Memory Gathers: Baseball and Poetry* (Rudi Publishing, 1998). He teaches at Carmel High School, Mundelein, Illinois.

MICHAEL WATERS's recent books include *Parthenopi: New and Selected Poems* (BOA Editions, 2001) and the seventh edition of *Contemporary American Poetry* (Houghton Mifflin, 2001). He teaches at Salisbury University on the Eastern Shore of Maryland.

DAVID WATTS, MD, is a clinical professor of medicine at the University of California, San Francisco, where he founded and runs the organization Poets on Parnassus. He has published three books of poetry, and he is also a commentator on National Public Radio's *All Things Considered*.

KYLE LEE WILLIAMS is a poet, writer, and scholar of comparative religion. She has taught at Hunter and Marymount Manhattan colleges in New York City. Her essays and scholarly articles have been published in *Lapis Magazine* and by the Archive for Research in Archetypal Symbolism.

HANNAH WILSON's work appears in *Caffeine Destiny, Calyx, Elysian Fields Quarterly, Prairie Schooner*, and elsewhere. A Literary Arts grant and residencies at Ragdale, Hedgebrook, and Centrum helped her complete a novel, *Soft Horizon*, as well as a collection of stories about old women.

JEFF WORLEY has published four collections of poetry, the most recent being *A Simple Human Motion* from Larkspur Press. His poems have appeared in over three hundred magazines and journals, including the *Threepenny Review, Poetry Northwest*, the *Georgia Review, New England Review, Shenandoah, DoubleTake*, the *Missouri Review*, and the *Southern Review*.

BARON WORMSER is the author of five books of poetry and the coauthor of *Teaching the Art of Poetry: The Moves*. He is the poet laureate of Maine and roots for the Baltimore Orioles.

KAREN ZABOROWSKI is the recipient of a New Jersey State Council on the Arts Fellowship in Poetry. Her work has appeared in numerous journals including *Calyx* and *Many Mountains Moving*. She teaches English at Atlantic City High School.

LARRY ZIRLIN works as a print production manager in New York. His poems have appeared in such journals as the *Paris Review*, the *World*, and *Hanging Loose*. The most recent of his four books is *Under the Tongue*.

BROOKE HORVATH teaches English at Kent State University. The author of two collections of poetry—*In a Neighborhood of Dying Light* and *Consolation at Ground Zero*—he has recently edited books on Henry James, William Goyen, George Garrett, and Thomas Pynchon. His poems, essays, and reviews have appeared in *American Literature, American Poetry Review, Antioch Review, Chicago Review, Denver Quarterly, Poetry,* the *Review of Contemporary Fiction, Tar River,* and elsewhere.

TIM WILES is the director of research at the National Baseball Hall of Fame and Museum in Cooperstown, New York. His baseball writings include a column, "Letters in the Dirt," available on the web, poems in *Elysian Fields Quarterly* and *Fan,* and numerous museum exhibits and Hall of Fame and Major League Baseball publications.